Traditional Literatures
of the American Indian

897
T7631   Traditional literatures
         of the American Indian

Traditional Literatures of the American Indian

Texts and Interpretations

Compiled and edited by
Karl Kroeber

University of Nebraska Press
Lincoln and London

First Bison Book Printing: 1981
Most recent printing indicated by first digit below:

1   2   3   4   5   6   7   8   9   10

Library of Congress Cataloging in Publication Data
Main entry under title:

Traditional literature of the American Indian.

1. Indian literature—North America—History and criticism—Addresses, es-
says, lectures. 2. Indians of North America—Legends—Addresses, essays,
lectures.
I. Kroeber, Karl, 1926–
PM155.T7   897   80–18338
ISBN 0–8032–2704–3
ISBN 0–8032–7753–9 pbk.

This book is dedicated to the memory of my parents

Alfred Louis Kroeber, 1876–1960
Theodora Kroeber Quinn, 1897–1979

Contents

Acknowledgments

Grateful acknowledgment is made to *Western American Literature* for permission to reprint Jarold Ramsey's essay, which originally appeared in that publication, as chapter 2 of this volume, and to the Columbia University Press, the Macmillan Company, the University of Chicago Press, the American Anthropological Society, and the Oregon Historical Society for permission to use material quoted in that chapter. Chapter 4 of this book, the essay by Barre Toelken and Tacheeni Scott, is based upon and expanded from Barre Toelken's "The Pretty Language of Yellowman," an article which first appeared in *Genre* and is used here by permission. And I am personally grateful to the University of California Press and the Columbia University Press for permission to reproduce here text and translation of the Kato "The Man Eater" and the Nez Percé "Red Willow" in this book's opening chapter.

KARL KROEBER

KARL KROEBER

An Introduction to the Art Of Traditional American Indian Narration

This book is intended to introduce nonspecialists to traditional American Indian literatures. Native Americans created a vast and remarkably diversified body of oral literatures, most of which has been lost through the destruction of Indian peoples and their cultures. Yet even what survives is impressive. The handful of stories in this volume cannot adequately represent the Native American literary accomplishment—which is still being carried forward today by new generations of Native American writers.[1] But I hope that these few tales with their accompanying commentaries will illuminate both the range and power of the literary achievements of the first Americans.

My experience teaching such material, however, has shown me that many Americans who know only Western literature are baffled by Indian oral narratives. Once in a while there is material familiar enough in theme, or dramatically enough structured, so that a modern Western reader spontaneously feels pleasure and excitement: the "Orpheus" tale in Jarold Ramsey's essay and the Coyote story recounted in Barre Toelken's essay exemplify these rare cases. But many Indian tales are not so accessible; and most create doubts, difficulties, and frustrations for a serious reader trying to understand in depth, wishing to gain something more than a superficial, and therefore patronizing, "appreciation" of Native American literary art.

Such a reader is likely to discover that there may be thousands of fine narratives preserved, but that they were recited (and recorded) in hundreds of different languages—for many of which there are neither grammars nor dictionaries, let alone native speakers, to be consulted. In brief, one is confined to translations, and of a kind which create a confluence of troubling questions. First, of course, one wonders, does this particular translation, perhaps by an anthropologist of no discernible skill as a writer of English, distort what the Indian teller said? And then, even if the translation is reasonably accurate, how can I, without any knowledge of the original language, recognize the subtleties which distinguish all literature? More specifically, one must ask if any *written* text can accurately produce an *oral* recitation. And, finally, perhaps, comes the query: Am I misreading this story because I am ignorant of the vanished culture in which it originated and which, to some degree, it reflects? The essays in this book cannot fully resolve such problems, but the commentaries will give an interested reader confidence to discover the rewards of carrying such questions into an active exploration of Indian narratives, rather than letting the difficulties prevent him from beginning.

An excellent starting place is the recognition that most of us, if we are inexperienced in Indian literatures, are not innocent and unprejudiced readers. We have been taught to read and to respond in particular ways to specific kinds of literary phenomena. It is not possible for most of us to react uninhibitedly (as young children may) to Indian stories. As a professional student of literature, I am peculiarly conscious of having lost such innocence. Innocence enabled me as a child to "correct" tellings to me of Yurok myths by Robert Spott, a full-blood Yurok. My "corrections" were based on earlier recitals to me by my anthropologist father. It is in keeping with what Dennis Tedlock and Barre Toelken say about oral performance in this volume that Robert was amused by my childish firmness in insisting he adhere exactly to my view of what were "authentic" versions of his sacred myths.

Very often it is not so much their unfamiliarity as our preconceptions that make it difficult for us to understand traditional Indian tales. So it helps an inexperienced reader to assume that such tales can be comprehended, that they are neither below nor beyond our customary procedures of analyzing and evaluating literature, and, therefore, that one should attack head-on any overt critical problems posed by a particular tale. One should begin by assuming that an Indian oral narrative may be a first-rate work of art. One must abandon the misconception that this literature is "primitive." It is not. It is worth remembering that all good literature raises troubling problems and is structured by intricacies which both attract and defeat the most intense analysis. I suggest that a reader unfamiliar with Indian materials first simply read through the stories in this volume (skipping the commentaries) and ask himself if his difficulties are not analogous to those he encounters with other kinds of excellent literary art.

In fact, Indian narratives *need* sophisticated critical attention. Literary critics would do well to follow the exhortation of a distinguished folklorist and student of Indian storytelling, Alan Dundes. Dundes wanted his fellow folklorists to tackle difficult materials courageously and to concentrate on discovering what he called "internal criteria" of three interacting "levels."[2] First, in Dundes's terminology, is *texture*, all features of verbal form, down to morphemes and phonemes. The second level he calls *text*, meaning one version of a single telling of a tale. Text, he points out, can be translated even when texture cannot; and he exemplifies this difference by a proverb, "Coffee boiled is coffee spoiled." One can conceive this text being translated easily enough, he says, but the chances for the survival of its principal textural feature, the rhyme, are slender. Dundes's third level is *context*: "the specific social situation in which the particular item is actually employed." Dundes separates context from "function," which he calls an abstraction fabricated by an observer from the study of a number of contexts. So "to say that a clan origin myth bolsters the ego of a clan [function] is not to say exactly how, when, where, to whom, and by whom the myth is uttered on a given specific occasion [context]."

Although Dundes thus distinguishes the level of context from text and texture, he does so because he believes that all three levels are necessary to a complete understanding of any folklore item. For this reason he urges folklorists not to abandon the analysis of texture to linguists, nor the analysis of context to anthropologists, because the other specialists cannot be sure of the significance of texts, the folklorists' particular province. Whether one is a linguist, anthropologist, or folklorist, he claims, a thorough understanding of any item derives only from an exploration of all three levels and their interrelations.

Now, anyone who has seriously studied any literature will recognize that exploration of the interrelations between what Dundes calls texture, text, and context is, in fact, what literary criticism is all about. When a critic encounters traditional Indian literatures, however, he must frequently work with a translated text lacking its original (hence without texture) and with little or no specific information about its context; therefore, literary analysis is by no means easy. But the critic must accept as even more applicable to him than to folklorists Dundes's caution not indolently to leave linguistic or anthropological problems of a text to be solved by specialists in other disciplines. Whether they know it or not, they need his expertise on its aesthetic features. By failing to struggle with Native American storytelling as an art, literary critics make more difficult the work of their colleagues. And the literary critic, because he is so concerned with the *relations* between what Dundes calls levels, can establish certain kinds of hypotheses which may advance the work of ethnologists, linguists, and folklorists.

To illustrate, I'll cite a brief, apparently simple story which seems only to pose a couple of minor problems of translation, that is, problems of texture in Dundes's terminology. I want to show that even so trivial a piece rewards critical attention. Of course, any literary judgment of this Kato tale must remain tentative so long as the underlying linguistic questions about it are not answered. Yet our difficulties in interpreting the story as literature will highlight some linguistic cruxes which a linguist might overlook. These cruxes, in turn, point to problems in context which an ethnologist might well not notice without the emphasis supplied by a literary critique. And for those interested solely in aesthetic matters, the very insufficiency of my preliminary comments points to how much adroit structuring actually underlies this seemingly artless tale.

The Man Eater

be L	na t goot Lon	ya'nee.	Le ne'ha'	na nesh	in che'
Rope /	they were tying /	they say. /	All /	persons /	deer/

on gee lang	ya'nee.	sah doong ha'	ts kaL	ya'nee.	t booL
went after /	they say. /	Alone /	she walked /	they say./	Basket/

ye geL   ya'nee.   toots   chh ghooL teeL   ya'nee.
she was carrying / they say. / Cane / she walked with /   they say. /

t booL   tallon   chh geL   ya'nee.   "sheeye'   inche'"
Basket /   soft /   she carried /   they say. /   "My /   deer"

chh in   ya'nee.   chh eL choot   ya'nee.   noon shoos teeng
she said / they say. / She caught him /   they say. /   She took him up

t booL bee'   noL teeng   ch'tesgeeng   ya'nee.
basket in /   she put him /   she carried him /   they say.

choongkeebo isch   o ye tah   wa ge goosh   t booL
Tree bent down /   under places /   carrying through /   basket /

noon chh ooL gal'   ochhoonga   ya'nee.   chh geL   ya'nee yeedookh.
she whipped /   over it /   they say. / She carried / they say / up hill. /

choong   oo yey   wa oong nging   choong   yeeL choot.
Tree /   under / she carried through /   tree /   he caught. /

da kit dool boosh.   woong ha   na goot daL   yee dookh.
He embraced it. /   Anyhow /   she went on /   up hill. /

noon chhooL gal'   toots   booL.   tshkon nes ne   chhin   ya'nee.
She whipped /   cane /   with. / She found out / she said (?) / they say./

na gool dal   hai da oong.   "sheeye'   inche'   tachee? "
She ran back /   down hill. /   "My /   deer /   where? " /

chhin   ya'nee.   deena nesh   da bes ya   choon khwoot.
she said / they say. / This man /   climbed on /   tree on. /

Loosh dee cho   chh ghooL tal   ya'nee.   sha   kasyai   ya'nee.
Rotten log /   she kicked /   they say. /   Sun /   came up /   they say. /

the'   kwna'   oo chhoong a   naL chos   ya'nee.
Blanket / her eyes /   over them /   she put /   they say. /

nee   ka no t yan   na heL'oots   ya'nee.   hai dookh   ya'nee.
She was ashamed. /   She ran back /   they say / here up /   they say. /

kwoon Lang
All. /

Free Version

    They were setting snares for deer. All the people had gone after deer.
He was walking alone. Some one was carrying a burden-basket. She was

walking along with a cane. She was carrying a soft burden-basket.

"My deer," she said. She caught him and put him in the basket. She carried him off. When she had to carry the basket under the branches of trees she whipped over her shoulder with her cane. She went east up the hill. When she went under a tree, he caught it and climbed up on it. She went on just the same, whipping with her cane. She found out what had happened. She ran back down the hill.

"Where is my deer?" she said.

The man climbed the tree. She kicked against a rotten log thinking he might be under it. The sun came up. She covered her face with her blanket because she was ashamed and ran up here east.

That is all.[3]

By providing both an interlinear and a free translation, Goddard displays visually how the very difficulties of translation may open a way for critical analysis. Most readers will be struck, I suspect, by the omission of "they say" from Goddard's free version. Whether he excluded his translation of *ya'nee* because he interpreted it as a phrase used by his informant only for the benefit of the ethnologist and not as part of a regular recitation, or whether he thought that, although a customary feature of myth recitations, it was distracting to the reader of his English text, Goddard does not say.[4] However, because *ya'nee* is used in other Kato myths Goddard recorded, but not in the one narrative of personal experience he transcribed (even though the experience was of a supernatural character), it seems probable that for Goddard's recitalist *ya'nee* has the effect of, "This is not my story, not a personal report, but a traditional, mythological event." But why should the assertion or disclaimer be repeated so often—either to Kato listeners or to a visiting anthropologist? One answer is that *ya'nee* is used as a rhythmic marker. It concludes each of the first ten sentences of "The Man Eater." In sentence 11 *ya'nee* appears for the first time in mid-sentence and then drops out as the man escapes, until the monster discovers her loss and speaks a second time. *Ya'nee* concludes the final five sentences, except the penultimate, and appears both in the middle and at the end of the last sentence. In other words, the formulaic element only twice interrupts sentences, at the halfway point, just before the man escapes as the monster moves off triumphantly, and at the end when she retreats in shamed and frustrated defeat. Such placings (along with the recitalist's closer association of *ya'nee* with the monster than with the man) illustrate how a textural feature also functions as a part of text structure, the double function allowing even a nonexpert to begin a literary interpretation, however tentative and unfinished.

An opposite approach, from text to texture, is illustrated by a discrepancy in Goddard's two versions of the third sentence, his interlinear version giving, "Alone she walked," as against his free version's, "He was walking alone." Can one imagine a Kato teller or Kato listener confusing victim with monster? Probably not, yet as one considers Goddard's slip, one may realize that isolation is a pervading theme in the tale. The man is isolated by being captured by the lone monster, who from the first is represented in contrast to "all persons" (Goddard tells us on page 71 that *na nesh* meant originally "human, not animal," though it came to distinguish "Indian" from "European"—another kind of monster), and whose shame at the end lies in being exposed by the sun as defeated. As one tries to evaluate the significance of the isolation motif, one increasingly encounters obstacles posed by the intense compression of the story. Not only is it brief, but it employs less than fifty distinct words. To interpret it, one must attend as carefully to its verbal nuances as one does with lyric poetry in our own tradition. Goddard's slip, therefore, is not minor, for each word and its place in "The Man Eater" seems carefully chosen, and each text-texture interrelation is but one part of a dense pattern of such interlockings.

An obvious instance of parallelism is provided by the monster's two speeches, when she finds and captures the man and when she discovers his escape. The economy of dramatic contrast here, moreover, is functional because the hunter-hunted inversion (refracting the group-isolate pattern) is inseparable from the whole set of contrastive parallelisms implicating text and texture within one another. For only one example I notice the interrelationship of "up-down" with "hard-soft" features. The tale begins with snares of woven rope for deer;[5] then a cane-carrying monster lifts the man and drops him into her woven back-basket, beating the tree branches with her cane until he escapes up a tree trunk. Discovering his flight on a hill, she rushes back down, vainly seeking him under a fallen, rotted tree. The sun rises, exposing her shame, and, raising her woven blanket over her face, she reverses direction, hastening away uphill. It is not difficult to perceive such patternings as reinforced and complicated by aural echoings and inversions. Thus the soft log the monster kicks (*chh ghooL tal*), though the man was never there, may aurally recall her entrance with hard cane (*chh ghooL teeL*) with which she twice "whips" (*noon chh ooL gal'*) down-bending trees, by means of one of which the man has escaped her. Analogously, the last sentence's final nonformulaic word *hai dookh* seems to recall by rhyme the endings of the plot-pivotal sentences 11 and 14, *yee dookh.*

Such comments are not intended to establish an interpretation of "The Man Eater." I simply want to suggest why it (like many Indian narratives) may usefully be regarded as a crafted, poetic artifact—even before we have the kind of formal structure Dell Hymes discovers as underlying the Clackamas story "Grizzly Woman Began to Kill People." My point is the elementary one that even an inexperienced reader can rewardingly apply to traditional Indian narratives the kind of critical attitude he brings to other literatures. When one does this, the primary discovery one makes is that *diversity* of interpretation is possible because the narrative truly is a work of art. In recognizing the story to be artistically shaped, one escapes the error of thinking that if we knew enough, say, about Kato culture we would automatically understand *the* meaning of "The Man Eater." So to believe is, however inadvertently, to treat the story as inferior, crude, "primitive." In fact, even when we have learned the Kato language and have understood as much as we can of the Kato culture from which "The Man Eater" emerges, we will still find room for conflicting readings and evaluations because it is a work of art. Each essay in this volume stresses, not ways of attaining a single definitive reading of a story or of a set of stories, but, instead, ways of entering into the rich complexity of meanings provided by traditional American Indian literary art.

It is worth remembering that if our limited linguistic and anthropological knowledge compels us to recognize that our first analyses of these stories must be tentative, our judgments provisional, and our evaluations speculative, an analogous inconclusiveness surrounds many texts in our own tradition. Much of the critical energy expended on the plays of Euripides, the romances of Chrétien de Troyes, and the novels of Defoe focuses on text-texture relations in order to establish what are *hypotheses* about context. With these works we can never legitimately claim a final or complete understanding. In constructing hypothetical relations between their texture, text, and context, we can only *improve* and *extend* our appreciation of the art of the writers and enrich our understanding of the cultures from which their works emerged. Exactly the same exploring processes are appropriate and rewarding for Indian literatures, although often we must start from more basic elements because Indian literatures lack the wealth of earlier studies with which Western works are surrounded. It is our scholarship, not Indian literature, which is "primitive" or undeveloped.

This is why one obstacle to appreciation of the literary merit of Indian stories, ironically, may be our awareness of our ignorance, especially of Indian cultures. That awareness, essential once we have begun systematically to study this material, may unnecessarily inhibit a first responsiveness, and sometimes encourages too solemn and reverential an attitude. A majority of Indian stories, whether scary like "The Man Eater" or humorous like the following "The Fawn, the Wolves, and the Terrapin," appeal to enough common features in human nature to allow us at least entrance to their pleasures—if only we can relax sufficiently to enjoy them.[6]

The Fawn, the Wolves, and the Terrapin

A beautiful Fawn met a Wolf one day who asked how he came to have such pretty spots over his body. "I got under a sieve and they put fire over it, and that made the pretty spots."

"Will you show me how I can do that?" asked the Wolf. The Fawn consented. Then the Wolf obtained a large sieve and lay down under it, and the Fawn built a fire and burned him to death. After the flesh had decayed, the Fawn took the bones of the back and made a necklace of them. One day the Fawn met a pack of Wolves, who said to him, "Where did you get that necklace?" But he refused to tell. "What is the song we hear you singing as you gallop over the prairie?" asked the Wolves. "If you will stand here till I get to the top of yonder hill I will sing it for you."

Ya-ha ya-ha	Wolf, wolf
Ef-oo-ne-tul	bones only
Chesarsook, chesarsook	rattle, rattle
Chesarsook	rattle
Kah-ke-tul	The ravens only
Methl-methl	fluttered, fluttered

Soolee-tul	The buzzard only
Methl-methl	fluttered, fluttered
Charnur-tul	The flies only
Sum-sum	buzzed, buzzed
Choon-tah-tul	The worms only
Witter-took	wiggled
Witter-took	wiggled
Witter-took.	wiggled.

When the Wolves heard this song they howled in anger and said: "We missed our mate. He is dead and those are his bones. Let us kill his murderer."

They started for the Fawn, who, seeing them, sped away for life, the bones rattling as he ran. He came to a basket maker and begged him to place him under a basket, but he refused. Then the Fawn came to a man who was getting bark to cover his house. "Oh, hide me from the Wolves," he begged, but the man would not. He ran on and came to a Terrapin who was making a spoon. "Tell me where to hide from the Wolves," said the Fawn. "No," replied the Terrapin, "I must not take sides." However, the Fawn saw a stream just ahead, and on reaching it he jumped up and lodged in the fork of a tree and could not extricate himself.

The Wolves passed the man who was making baskets and the man who was getting bark to cover his house and came to the Terrapin, who told them the way Fawn had gone.

When the Wolves reached the stream, they could trace the Fawn no farther. They looked in the water, and there they saw him. They tried to go into the water to catch the Fawn but failed. In sorrow they began to howl. As they raised their heads in howling, they saw the Fawn in the tree. One Wolf said, "I know a man who can shoot him out"; so he sent for the man. Then he went to the Terrapin and brought him, and the Terrapin said he could kill him. He began to shoot arrows at the Fawn. He shot every arrow away and missed the Fawn. Afterwards, while walking around the tree, Terrapin found one of his old arrows sticking in the ground near an old log. "This was one of my best arrows," said he. So he shot at the Fawn and with this old arrow killed him.

Then the Wolves took the body and divided it into pieces. "We must pay the man for shooting him," one said, so they offered the Terrapin a piece of one leg. But he had some complaint in his leg, and the medicine men had told him not to eat the leg of any animal. He whined out, "I cannot eat leg; it will make my leg hurt, and I shall die."

When they offered him a shoulder, he whined out, "I cannot eat shoulder; it will pain my shoulder, and I shall die."

"He does not want any," they said, and went away carrying all of the Fawn.

After they had gone, the Terrapin looked around and saw that there was blood on the leaves; so he gathered the bloody leaves into a big bundle, saying, "I'll carry them home." He reached his house, threw down the bundle, and said to his wife, "There, cook it for the children." Then she unrolled the bundle but saw nothing. "Where is it?" she asked. "Way inside," replied he; so she separated the leaves, but finding nothing but blood, she threw it in his face. He called to the children to bring him some water; but as they were slow, he crawled around with his eyes closed and found the lye and washed his face in that. Some of this got in his eyes and made them red, and ever since terrapins have had red eyes.

This entertaining narrative appears in a collection of translations unaccompanied by originals or ethnographic commentary. For the nonspecialist, then, the tale lacks texture or context. Fortunately, John R. Swanton does provide a transliteration of the Fawn's song, so one may begin with it as a clue to the textural elements obscured by translation. The song is markedly onomatopoetic—even to our ears *methl-methl* and *sum-sum* may have the sound of fluttering wings and buzzing flies. And as we learn from a note of Swanton's, the song seems to distort the normal form of words, so that the onomatopoeia appears part of a kind of aural joking. Such lightheartedness may justify a speculation that *witter-took* humorously imitates the worms. Yet the song is not just silly. After the jeering *ya-ha ya-ha* address to the Wolves, the bones, whose tripled rattle (*chesarsook*) rhymes with the concluding worms' tripled wriggling (*witter-took*), are succeeded by three doublets interlinked by the rhymed "only" (*tul*). It seems a reasonable guess that the surrounding tale may also exploit verbal ingenuity through careful structuring to attain diverse humorous effects.[7]

Although the tale at first appears only a string of episodes, it is in actuality cleverly arranged to emphasize progressively without mere repetition a theme of the fooling fool fooled. Credulous, envious Wolf gets himself burned to a crisp. His victimizer, Fawn, achieves a good start on Wolf's brothers though Fawn hasn't been able to resist either an appeal to his looks or the opportunity for a taunting brag—quite in accord with his vanity in wearing the doubly fatal necklace. Fawn catches himself, absurdly, in a tree. Witlessly plunging after his image (reflecting Fawn's vanity?), the Wolves howl in frustration, and in raising their heads accidently discover the self-trapped Fawn. In line with their foolishness, their council solicits the aid of the biggest incompetent available. Terrapin's vanity has a less factual basis than Fawn's; but by the improbable chance of finding a long-lost (so presumably crooked) arrow, he does kill Fawn for the bumbling Wolves. Then, greedily trying to scrounge more of the carcass than he's offered, Terrapin does himself out of any food at all. At this point the narrative turns domestic, with Terrapin's effort to impose on his wife earning him a faceful of bloody leaves. And his error with the lye attains for him the permanent discomfort of red eyes, a fitting conclusion for a tale beginning with a wolf seeing spots.

This quick-paced, amusing narrative, its humor varying from the slapstick of leaves-in-the-face to the sly contrast of the dishonest Terrapin to the honest house-builder and basket-maker, needs no laborious analysis. But we shouldn't overlook the skill with which we are carried forward from Fawn-Wolf rivalry to Terrapin as inept paterfamilias, self-deceiving and finally self-injuring, so as to recall the original Wolf's (and Fawn's) self-destruction. The circularity of the tale's form seems to echo the circularity of the Fawn's song, and it appears that a perception by the audience of the deft artistry of their relationship is intended. At any rate, pleasure in such arrangement formally reinforces the shrewd perceptiveness of the tale's "message": this is a world well supplied with vain and greedy fools. It may be chance that the story seems without specialized cultural or religious reference, but the easy skill of the narration along with the broadly humane morality surely reveal something about the nature of the people who enjoyed telling it and hearing it: these were not morose savages killing time around a smoky fire.

It is difficult to conceive of such a relaxedly elegant narrative occurring in a society without an appreciation of expert artistry. Indeed, it is not easy to find a parallel from our own literature to the brilliantly economical characterization of Terrapin, the braggart-liar type who in trying to cheat everyone else inevitably cheats himself. Whatever the special circumstances in which "The Fawn, the Wolves, and the Terrapin" was originally told, whatever its context, and whatever riches of texture have been lost in translation, in the English text alone there are pleasures for anyone of ironic intelligence who can take satisfaction in a well-made verbal artifact and who has some appreciation for the perpetual absurdities of human behavior. In sum, in this Creek story we have artistry no more "primitive" than Chaucer's in, say, "The Miller's Tale."

But even if we find "The Fawn, the Wolves, and the Terrapin" worthwhile, and even if we are willing to recognize that the society which produced and enjoyed such a tale possessed sophistication of no mean order, we may still be reluctant to admit the degree to which such art manifests a profound and significant *self*-understanding. Self-consciousness we feel to be a prerogative of our art. We like, naturally enough, to think our own art is best, and that only we have a developed, self-aware comprehension of sociocultural dynamics. Yet the essays in this volume reveal how much capacity for self-analysis Native American storytellers and listeners possessed. And once we can accept the possibility of a challenge to our critical ethnocentrism, we will find a new dimension of aesthetic meaning in Indian tales, one which makes them extraordinarily valuable for understanding not only their contexts but also, by implication, the fashion in which most cultures work. A Nez Percé tale will illustrate the point.

píplaats
Red Willow

kaálaa	awáka		laáwtiwaa		hatá'aw		ta'áXatoom.
Just /	it was his /		comrade /		very dear /		a youth's. /

timaáy	hiwákaa.	kawó'	yoq'	opí	timaáy	hiwáyatoo.
A maiden /	she was. /	Then /	That /	maiden /	went in quest of a vision. /

"poótimt	láhayn	koósa	kaa	ts'aalwí	wát'oo'
"Ten /	days /	I am going /	and /	if /	not /

paáytoqo'	a	nakoó'	waáqo'	koo'itoónm	póptsiown."
I return /	you /	will think /	already /	something /	kills her." /

mát'oo	kii	oos	táwtiwa.	Kaawó'	hiwi'nana	kaa
But /	here /	hers is /	fiancé. /	Then /	she went /	and /

pátwixna	ta'áxatoom.	pátwixna	kaa	konaá	póptsiaawnaa
he followed her /	the youth. /	He followed her /	and /	there /	he killed her /

ta'áxatoom.	waliímtsaapki	pá'wiya.	wát'oo'	mína
the youth. /	With an arrow /	he shot her. /	Not /	anywhere /

paánixqaanaa   tsápna.   pásapalooxqaanaa   kaa   hikóqaanaa
could he put /   the arrow. / He would hide it /   and /   go away /

kaa   koónk'oo'   paáxnaaqaanaa   kaálaa   xaa'aáw   hilaaXaáwtsaa
and / always /   he would see it /   just /   a red glow / burning red /

íska   kiká't.   óykaakaapaa / hisapaloóka   máťoo   koónk'oo'
like / blood. / At all places / he hid it / but /   always /

paáxnaaqaanaa   kaálaa   hilaaxaá'aawtsaa.   konaá   hihína,
he would see it /   just /   glowing red. /   There /   he said, /

"iyó!   taamaawiín.   mínax   aawnikaáX? "   kiímat   kaa
"Confound it! / It is too much. /   Where / shall I put it? " / When /   then

konmaá   pawstooka'áyka   tsápna   kaa   konó'
over that way /   he shot it /   the arrow /   and /   there

hitqapalakapaya   píplaatspaa.   kaa   wáťoo'   mína   páxna
it stuck amid /   willows. /   And /   not /   anywhere / he saw it. /

kii   kaawó'   hitskilíyna   kaa   konaá   hiwíynaaqaanaa,
Now /   then /   he went home /   and /   there /   he would weep, /

"iínim   ootáwtiwa,   iínim   ootáwtiwa."   kaa   ipnátsa,
"My /   fiancée, /   my /   fiancée." /   And / saying to himself, /

"miŕsax   hipaamaáynaaX,   ipním   póptsiaawnaa."
"How could it be of me / they would suspect me, / that he / killed her." /

ku'ús   hiwanípa,   kaálaa   hiwíytsa.   kaa   oos   aásqaap,
Thus / he sang, /   just /   he is weeping. / And / his is / younger brother, /

kaálaa hiXaláwisa,   ipnaataamqitaayítsaa   tsápki   kaa
just / he plays /   spearing targets /   with arrows /   and /

hiwanpís ipínk'oo',   "iínim   ootáwtiwa,   iínim   ootáwtiwa."
he sings / he, too, /   "My /   fiancée, /   my /   fiancée." /

kii   ipnaatXtaayítsaa   kaa   pikápim   paña,   "maanaámaa
Here /   he spears targets /   and /   his mother / said to him, / "What is

yoX   ku'ús   hitátoo? "   "kaálaa naa'yaátsaap   aamts'iítaato
that / thus / you keep saying? " / "Just / my elder brother / I often hear

hiwanptátoo   kaa   kaálaa   asapálapsqooyasa."   pikápim
he sings often /   and / just / I am imitating him." /   His mother /

kii   pána   pisítna ,   "waáqo' paays   áta   póptsiaawnaa."
here / said to him, / the father, / "Now / probably / it is that / he killed her." /

átka waáqo hikóqaanaa poótimt láhayn; kaa waáqo
Because / now / he would go / ten / days / and / now /

timaáynim pîka hiwíynima. kaa hilaXsáXtsa, hisaayóXo'saa
the maiden's / mother / wept / And / opens wide her mouth, / looks /

maqsámkinkayx ka konmá akoóya paáhaap. (áta
toward the mountain / that which / way / hers went / daughter. / (It was that

ta'áxatoom kaakaá póptsiaawnaa, timaáyina hoókux
the youth / when / he killed her, / the maiden's / hair /

paasaak'iíwkaa'nyaa kaa yoq'opî hinápta kaakaá hiwanpísa,
he had cut hers off / and / that / he holds / while / he sings,

ha'átXawtsa mat hitilaáptsaa.) kaawó' hiwíynima aátwaay,
deeply grieves / but also / longs.) / Then / she wept / the old woman, /

kii / ku'ús hiXsáxtsa hiwíytsa. kiîmat tsilyáxnim
like / this / she opens wide her mouth / she weeps. / Thereupon / a fly

q'o' ts'aa'aá' him poóyayalaka'nya kaa q'o'
precisely / true / her mouth / it flew into / and / at once /

pátqakanpa tsilyáxna —— t'uks q'o' tsilyáxna;
she bit it / the fly / —— burst open / thereupon / the fly; /

isiímat maátsi'n, kaa ipnána aátwaay, "waá'qu'
behold / fetid, / and / she said to herself / the old woman, / "Already /

átax ti'nxniín was miyaá'ts." kaawó' pá'pawisana
it is that mine / dead / is / child." / Then / they searched for her /

timaáyinaa átka waáqo' aátwaaynim oýkaalonaa hinásna,
the maiden / because / now / the old woman / all of them / said to them, /

"ti'nxniín hiíwas." kaa hipakoóya maqsámkax
"Dead / she is." / And / they went / to the mountains

pá'pawisana. kaawó' kii paáyaaXtsaanaa. áta inakiíx
looking for her. / Then / here / they found her. / It was that / even

pawawiíka mát'oo paáyaaXtsaanaa kaa páxtsana áta
he had buried her / but / they found her / and / they saw / that /

awyiín hiíwas, kaa pá pawisana itoóki pá'awya.
shot / she is, / and / they searched for that / with which / he had shot her. /

q'o' tsaáyaa tsap mîna. óykaaslix hipaasaayóXo'yaa,
Absolutely / absent / arrow / anywhere. / All about / they searched, /

q'o' wát'oo' maáwaa tsápna paáyaaXtsaanaa. kii
absolutely / not / ever / the arrow / they found. / Here /

15

hipanáxtsixliyka	tsilaáxt	kaa	konaá	patamiksána	kaa
they took home /	the body /	and /	there /	they buried her /	and /

wát'oo'	maáwaa	hipatsoóxwana	isiiñm	póptsiaawnaa,
not /	ever /	they found out /	who /	killed her /

átka	wát'oo'	tsap	paáyaaXnaaysaanaa.	konix	hiwts'áya
because /	not /	arrow /	they found his. /	From there /	it became /

píplaats	ilp'ilp,	timaáynim	kikát.
willow /	red, /	the maiden's /	blood. /

Free Translation

A youth had a very dear comrade (and fiancée)—a maiden. It came to pass that the maiden went in quest of a vision. "I am going for ten days, and if I do not return, then you will know that something has killed me." Here was her fiancé, and when she went this youth followed her. He followed and killed her; shot her with an arrow. He could find no place to put the arrow. He tried to hide it, but always on going away he could see it glowing red, glowing like blood. He hid it in many places, but always he would see the red glow. There he said to himself, "Confound it! This is too much. Where shall I place it?" Thereupon he shot the arrow away and it stuck amid willows, and he saw it no more. Now he went home. There he began to weep, "My fiancée, my fiancée." But to himself he would say, "How could they suspect me of killing her? " Thus he sang and wept. He had a younger brother who played about, spearing targets with arrows; and he, too, now began to sing, "My fiancée, my fiancée." Here he was spearing targets when his mother said to him, "What is this you say constantly? "—"I am only imitating my elder brother; I hear him sing often." The mother now said to his father, "It is likely that he has killed her." They had noticed, also, that he would go away for ten-day periods. Now the maiden's mother wept, opening wide her mouth, and looked toward the mountain to which her daughter had gone. (It was that when the youth had killed the maiden, he had cut off her hair; and this hair he clutched as he sang, deeply grieving and longing.) The old woman, the maiden's mother, wept. She wept with her mouth open, and a fly flew directly into it. She bit down on the fly quickly and burst it open; behold, the fly was fetid. She said to herself, "My child is already dead." Then a search was made for the maiden because the old woman had announced, "She is dead." They went to the mountains to search for the body. There they found it where he had even tried to bury the maiden; they found her and saw that she had been shot. They searched for the arrow with which she had been shot, but there was none to be found. They searched all about, but never did they find the arrow. They took the maiden's body home and buried it there. They never found out who had killed her because the arrow was never found. From that it came to pass that the willow is red—of the maiden's blood.[8]

The obvious question posed by this tale is why the young man killed his fiancée. Because this is an Indian story, the modern reader tends to answer by speculating on the possible relevance of tribal customs, taboos, and special rites. We seek assistance in our anthropological information. But we might better consider (as literary critics normally incline to do with more familiar material) a possibility that to the Nez Percés themselves the young man's action may have been "mysterious." For the Nez Percés, too, the puzzle of motive may have been the point of this story. The possibility strengthens the more we become aware of the ramifying intricacy of ambivalences in "Red Willow."

Quite simply, again, we have to hypothesize that this troubling story is a work of art. After all, the presentation of mysterious motive has long been recognized as a legitimate prerogative for artists in our own literary tradition. Why the youth kills his fiancée, I propose, may be a deliberately unanswered question, one intended to compel the recitalist's audience to confront dark mysteries of the human heart. All the supposition entails is granting the creators of "Red Willow" artistic capabilities and ambitions not inferior to those of a literary artist in our society. To some, I fear, such a comparison may still seem radical. Our critics seldom find any works outside the modern Western tradition worth more than cursory attention. Anthropologists and folklorists, whose disciplines are not directed toward appreciation of superior artistry, usually play down, or ignore, the individual distinction of creative accomplishment in ethnographic material.[9] But a story such as "Red Willow" *is* unusual; and if we concentrate on its unusualness, we may discover how aesthetic analysis can contribute even to an ethnological understanding.

A literary critic probably will be struck by the circumstance that there is no way of being certain *to* whom the maiden speaks in the fourth sentence of "Red Willow." Following the clue of that doubtfulness, he will notice that shifts in addressee seem to be significant in the story; for instance, the murderer and his victim's mother, surprisingly, are alike in speaking to themselves.

An anthropologist is more likely to observe that the maiden seeks a guardian spirit, such a quest being the central religious practice of the Nez Percés.[10] That these apparently unconnected observations do interrelate one can demonstrate by following through the speaker-addressee patterns in the story, even in simplified fashion. The young man speaks primarily to himself, in a way appropriately, since he appears a divided personality. But his "private" lamentation is meant to deceive the tribe at large, though, ironically, the echo of his words by his younger brother crystallizes his mother's suspicion, which she voices only to her husband, the young man's father. Undeceived, she does not reveal the truth to the tribe. The maiden's mother, however, first speaks to herself, but then to the tribe, sending them out to find her daughter's body, though not the identity of the killer. The combination of contrast and parallelism is reflected in various ironies. Thus, to cite but one point, the murderer remains undetected because the fatal weapon is not located, even though the natural world continues to "proclaim" its place of concealment through the red willow plant—even as the traditional story itself continues to "disclose" what was unknown with certainty to all but the youth. "Red Willow" is, in both the most obvious and the most subtle sense, a disclosure of mystery.

Intricate interplayings of concealment and revelation serve a definite, if paradoxical, purpose. That the tribe fails to discover the murderer, although through the tribal tradition of the story itself the anonymous protagonist (that is to say, anyone) is "identified" as the murderer, illuminates our "difficulty" in understanding the motive of the killer. We *do* understand the young man's motivations, but we are hesitant to identify them. We desire to deceive ourselves, as the youth deceives himself when he exults that his public laments conceal his criminality: "How could they suspect me of killing her?"[11] His deliberately misleading public declaration inadvertently expresses a true anguish he feels, physically evidenced by the hair he cut from the girl's head. As with his compulsive reenactment of his fiancée's quest, he grieves for the loss of what he has made to disappear. And as he tries to cling to what he had destroyed, his younger brother "playing," that is, shooting at a target rather than at real *game* (the pun in English reflecting, I think, the ambiguities with which the story is concerned), unwittingly betrays the crime to their parents. If this seems to "read in" too much psychological subtlety, I would defend the interpretation by pointing to how the echoed lament precipitates suspicion in the mother's mind. We might have difficulty explaining the psychic process, but surely for us as for her the repeated conjunction of the words "My fiancée, my fiancée" just as an arrow plunges into its target might initiate an unprovable yet certain intuition. Every detail reveals "Red Willow" to be a narrative carefully structured through inversions and reflections to enable a listener to explore self-concealed psychic impulses.

This structuring involves text and texture, as in the younger brother's "reflecting" his elder's situation, which is reinforced by a linguistic detail. The story's opening *kaalaa* recurs in sentences 10 and 11, when the murderer cannot hide the deadly arrow, and then again as he weeps in sentence 19 just before his younger brother appears. *Kaalaa* is used again in the next sentence, and the first involving the younger brother, and reappears for the *last* time in the story as the introductory element of the two clauses in the younger brother's unconsciously revealing speech as his arrows strike home (sentence 22).

Other rhetorical/linguistic details help to make efficacious the psychological complexities in the story. There is, for example, the intrusion of the young man's false/true grieving in the midst of the report of the maiden's mother's lament, the intrusion reinforcing the ironic link between characters who speak to themselves. And one may notice the adroit placing of *kii*, which Archie Phinney usually translates as "here," but which would seem more accurately rendered in English by "now," since it always points up a critical *moment* of action or revelation,[12] as in sentence 35 when the reburial of the girl marks the tribe's definitive failure to discover her murderer. A final instance: the putrid fly, which shoots "precisely true," *a'o' ts'aa'aa',* into the mother's mouth from the mountain (so revealing the daughter's first burial place) is inversely echoed by the "absolutely absent," *q'o' tsaayaa,* arrow (which *could* have disclosed the murderer). Among reasons for this kind of careful textural paralleling is the obvious one that the foul insect in the mother's mouth "speaks" loudly not only to the place and condition of the girl's body but also to the corruption in the lover/killer.

Even these few observations point to the remarkable artistry with which "Red Willow" is shaped, an artistry *necessary* because the story treats of what is difficult to discuss openly, difficult even for an individual to think about himself. Like all good works of literature, the story does not merely illustrate a convention- alized attitude toward a particular phenomenon nor simply re- state a familiar taboo, but, instead, explores and dramatizes the tensions out of which arise cultural attitudes, beliefs, presupposi- tions, and restrictions. The vision quest on which the girl sets out is, as anthropologists tell us, a central feature of Nez Percé reli- gion. Both young boys and girls sought guardian spirit visions by going alone on fasting vigils into remote mountain areas. I have not found any ethnographic discussion of what sometimes must have occurred in those dangerous circumstances, possibilities to which "Red Willow" speaks so vividly and poignantly. The tale, in fact, articulates in psychologically and socially effective fashion some deep psychic tensions which necessarily derive from the Nez Percés' intense seeking after supernatural aid. Such articu- lating does not undermine their religion. To the contrary, "Red Willow" renders it more significant. The story proves that the Nez Percés did not conceal from themselves the inner dangers of the religious quest-vision—dangers about which our anthropologists have been silent. More specifically, the story dramatizes the destructive inner impulses which it is the successful guardian spirits' function to reorient into constructive channels. We cer- tainly need a knowledge of Nez Percé religion to understand "Red Willow." But just as certainly we need to appreciate the story as a fine work of art if we are to comprehend the dynamics of Nez Percé religiosity. Not until we learn to recognize the artistry of American Indian literatures will we find direct routes toward a more than superficial (and inevitably rather formalistic) anthro- pological understanding.

The essays in this book are intended to enable a reader to recognize artistry in American Indian narratives. Jarold Ramsey's presentation of a lovely Orphic story from the Nez Percés first of all calls attention to the richness of the delicate yet powerful literary procedures employed by the recitalist. These include symmetrical structuring, prefiguration, and highly focused dra- matic speech and gesture. But Ramsey goes beyond simple descrip- tion. He compares the brilliant dramatization of two parallel tales, showing how each is built around a different but equally profound articulation of human frailties and desires. And then, further defining the unique quality of his Nez Percé myth, Ramsey points out how in the surprising final episode, "the narrative seems to move beyond the modes and logic of myth *per se,* assuming a status more like that of fiction—as if Coyote has now entered *our* kind of reality."[13]

The second contributor to this volume is Dennis Tedlock, who presents not an essay but a dramatization, or enactment, of how the Zuni beginning happens. Tedlock demonstrates how a Zuni storyteller is necessarily an interpreter because Zuni telling and interpreting interpenetrate. He shows that a Zuni story *continues* precisely because each reciter is a reviser. This dialectical role reflects dialectics in the story, like that of time, as when we encounter the coexistence of the apparently mutually exclusive periods of four years and four days for the protagonists' first stop on their way to the place of the modern Zuni. Even more impressive is the dialectical defining of the protagonist twins, who are named only by reference to each other, "the Ahayuuta's elder brother" and "the Ahayuuta's younger brother." So, as Tedlock puts it, "what is called Ahayuuta is between them." And, though they mark the beginning, they always already have a grandmother—"of course," named "Ahayuuta's grandmother" or, in Tedlock's words, "Grandmother of difference." One thing we can be certain of when we finish Tedlock's revelation of how Zuni text and interpretation are always already there is that only the most sophisticated of critical procedures, *extending* the conceptions of Paul Ricoeur and Martin Heidegger, will be adequate to the subtlety of Zuni art and interpretation.

Barre Toelken with the aid of Tacheeni Scott demonstrates not merely how a Native American recitalist actually tells a story but also how his audience responds to and participates in the telling. Toelken, furthermore, elucidates the significance of these events. One passage, for example, dramatizes with precision the complexity of narrative's sustaining function in Native American cultures:

Why, then, if Coyote is such an important mythic character (whose name must not even be mentioned in the summer months), does Yellowman tell such funny stories about him? Yellowman's answer: "They are not funny stories." Why does everyone laugh, then? "They are laughing at the way Ma'i does things, and at the way the story is told. Many things about the story are funny, but the story is not funny." Why tell the stories? "If my children hear the stories, they will grow up to be good people; if they don't hear them, they will turn out to be bad." Why tell them to adults? "Through the stories everything is made possible."

Toelken goes on to demonstrate through a lucid reanalysis and retranslation of an earlier study of the Navajo story that in Indian narrative art, "'meaning,' really, is no more *in* the texture than it is *in* the structure," for "structure and texture unite to provide an excitement of meaning which already exists elsewhere, in the shared ideas and customs of people raised in an intensely traditional society." Coyote stories act like "surface structure" in language: "By their articulation they touch off a Navajo's deeper accumulated sense of reality; they excite perspectives on truth by bringing a 'critical mass' together which is made up of ethical opposites . . . so complicated and profound that vicarious experience in it through entertainment is one of the only access points available to most people."

In the final essay Dell Hymes dramatizes how crucial to anyone seeking such access is sensitivity to the aesthetic uses of linguistic details. Hymes illustrates how an apparently trivial variation in the prefix to noun stems is in fact a key to understanding both the structure and meaning of Clackamas stories. Hymes's analysis is the most intricate and difficult in this volume, not because he deals in detail with an unfamiliar language, but because he treats a subtlety whose difficult significance is characteristic of the aesthetic orderings of language in all superior literary works. What Hymes discovers about the form of "Grizzly Woman Began to Kill People," that the dramatic center of the story "will be found to involve the stylistic choice of whether and where to name, and if to name, then how," is true, mutatis mutandis, of much literary narration, as modern critics such as Ian Watt, Roland Barthes, and Wolfgang Iser have observed. We must learn to recognize that the kind of detailed preciseness of Hymes's scholarship is ultimately what Native American literatures *require* if their rich significancy is to be appreciated. It is my hope that the sequence of essays in this book will lead readers to develop an understanding of both the challenges and the profound rewards offered by serious attention to American Indian literary accomplishments.

Notes

1. Among whom one may mention novelists N. Scott Momaday, *House Made of Dawn*; James Welch, *Winter in the Blood* (and a collection of poems, *Riding the Earthboy 40*); Leslie Marmon Silko, *Ceremony*; and poets such as Ray Youngbear and Simon Ortiz. For reviews, criticism, and bibliographic data on Native American writers, consult the *Newsletter* of the Association for the Study of American Indian Literatures, issued from Columbia University.

2. Alan Dundes, "Texture, Text, and Context," *Southern Folklore Quarterly* 28, no. 4 (December 1966): 251-65. The following quotations are from pp. 255-56.

3. Text and translations are from Earle Pliny Goddard, "Kato Texts," *University of California Publications in American Archaeology and Ethnology* 5, no. 3 (Berkeley: 1907-10), pp. 65-238, 179-80, 235-36. Goddard's description and analysis of the Kato language will be found in volume 11 (1912) of the same series. I have made the following changes in Goddard's orthography of the Kato text: *a* as in *father* = *aa*; *i* as in *pique* = *ee*; *u* as in *rule* = *oo*; his *q* to *k*; his *c* for *sh* in *shall* to *sh*; his *j* as *z* in *azure* to *zh*; his *G* as in German *Tag* to *gh*; his *dj* as *j* in *juice* to *j*; and his *tc* and *tc'* (aspirated and unaspirated surds corresponding to his *dj*) to *ch* and *chh*, an added *h* for strong aspiration; ' for glottal stop, and *X* for a velar voiceless fricative, and *L* for "voiceless l" like Welsh *ll*.

4. Compare Toelken's discussions of this formulaic element below.

5. We probably think of a noose for feet (hunting from below), but I suspect the Katos were more likely to use a neck noose, the different possibilities illustrating how the interpenetration of literary and ethnological problems may carry one toward problems of context.

6. The text below is from John R. Swanton, *Myths and Tales of the Southeastern Indians*, Bureau of American Ethnology Bulletin no. 88 (Washington, D.C.: GPO, 1929), pp. 38-40, very slightly modified, e.g., I have substituted "sieve" for the regional "riddle." The original collector, W. O. Tuggle, specified that the teller was a woman, and there may be an element of feminine ridicule of masculinity. Changes in the song words noted by Swanton include *Ef-oo-ne* for *ifoni* ("bone"), *methl-methl* for *milmil* ("flutter"), and *sum* for *sam* ("buzz").

7. Many Indian stories incorporate songs, but there has been little study of the formal interrelatings of the two modes—another evidence of the primitiveness of our scholarship.

8. Archie Phinney, *Nez Percé Texts*, Columbia University Contributions to Anthropology, vol. 25 (New York: Columbia University Press, 1934), pp. 173-76. For details on Phinney and his collection see Ramsey's essay

below. I have followed Phinney's orthography for the Nez Percé except for using (as with the Kato text above) *aa, ee, oo* for vowels *a* as in *father, i* as in *pique,* and *u* as in *rule,* and *X* and *L* as described in note 2. The apostrophe indicates glottalization of the preceding sound, and the accent indicates stress, which Phinney says is crucial to rhythm (p. xi). Phinney's description of the sounds of other letters used is as follows (p. x): *a* = *man*; *i* = *it*; *o* = *no*; *u* = *full*; *w* = *wet*; *y* = *yet*; *h* = *had*; *x* = voiceless mid-palatal continuant; *k* = aspirated mid-palatal plosive; *q* = voiceless velar plosive; *l* = voiced *l*; *p* = aspirated bilabial plosive; *t* = aspirated plosive; *ts* = alveolar affricative; *s* = voiced bilabial nasal; *n* = voiced alveolar nasal.

9. Lévi-Straussian structuralism has, of course, encouraged the tendency to disregard unique qualities in oral narratives.

10. See, for example, Herbert Joseph Spinden, "The Nez Percé Indians," *Memoirs of the American Anthropological Association,* no. 2, pt. 3 (1907-15): 165-274.

11. In sentence 18 of the free translation a complexity is lost as the youth speaking to himself slides from subjectivity ("How could it be of me they would suspect me") toward the position of the deceived group ("that he killed her").

12. Phinney's text demonstrates that the story was *recited*, meant to be "acted out" as told: sentences 15, 21, and 27 ("like this" and "behold") *require* gestural action in conjunction with the telling.

13. For another example of narrative deconstruction in a Transformer myth in a Wishram Coyote cycle, see my essay "Deconstructionist Criticism and American Indian Literatures," *Boundary 2,* vol. 7, no. 3 (Spring 1979): 73-92.

JAROLD RAMSEY

From "Mythic" to "Fictive" in a Nez Percé Orpheus Myth

The Orphic story, of a hero's unsuccessful quest to bring back a loved one from the Land of the Dead, is apparently universal among American Indian tribes.[1] In its permutations, the story has a powerful intrinsic appeal that transcends cultural barriers, speaking to us all as mortal humans; and when looked at as oral literature, many of the Indian Orpheus stories reveal, even at the double remove of transcription into print and translation, a striking degree of narrative artistry, as if their anonymous creators were conscious of rising to the occasion of a great theme.

Of such myths, surely one of the most compelling is the Nez Percé "Coyote and the Shadow People," recorded and translated by Archie Phinney in Lapwai, Idaho, in 1929. Now, Phinney's texts are of special value in the study of traditional Western Indian literature because they were collected and edited under nearly perfect conditions. Phinney was a Nez Percé himself, educated at Columbia University and trained in ethnography and linguistics by Franz Boas; and when he returned to the Lapwai Reservation he took as his sole informant his own mother, "Wayi-latpu," a gifted storyteller who spoke no English, and whose knowledge of her repertory, Phinney tells us, extended back three generations and therefore "beyond the time when the influences of new intertribal contacts and of wholesale myth-trading at non-reservation Indian schools became apparent in Nez Perce mythology."[2]

In terms of classical Boasian scholarship, then, it would be hard to improve upon Phinney's circumstances—they are probably unique among Far Western Indians—and it is clear from his textual work that he brought to it an unusual combination of editorial rigor and literary sensitivity. His translations aim at the more-than-literal recreation in English of stylistic features in the original narratives; there is a kind of *elegance* to them, which, to be sure, now and then does strike a somewhat stilted Latinate note, but which, overall, seems appropriate to stories as rich as these. One of Phinney's great virtues, I think, is his constant awareness of what can be lost in transforming the drama of oral narrative into print—lines on a page. As he complained in a letter to Boas: "A sad thing in recording these animal stories is the loss of spirit—the fascination furnished by the peculiar Indian vocal tradition for humor. Indians are better story-tellers than whites. When I read my story mechanically I find only the cold corpse."[3]

The final sentence of Phinney's introduction to his collection is an eloquent plea—one worth heeding now as we set out to examine just one of his people's stories—against reading the stories mechanically, out of context, and for, instead, opening the imagination to them as a mythology. He says: "Any substantial appreciation of these tales must come not from the simple elements of drama unfolded but from vivid feeling within oneself, feeling as a moving current all the figures and the relationships that belong to the whole mythbody."[4]

Now for the story, "Coyote and the Shadow People"——

Coyote and his wife were dwelling there. His wife became ill. She died. Then Coyote became very, very lonely. He did nothing but weep for his wife.

There the death spirit came to him and said, "Coyote, do you pine for your wife?" — "Yes, friend, I long for her. . . ." replied Coyote. "I could take you to the place where your wife has gone, but, I tell you, you must do everything just exactly as I say; not once are you to disregard my commands and do something else." — "Yes," replied Coyote, "yes, friend, and what else could I do? I will do everything you say." Then the ghost told him, "Yes. Now let us go." Coyote added, "Yes, let it be so that we are going."

They went. There he said to Coyote again, "You must do whatever I say. Do not disobey." — "Yes, yes, friend. I have been pining so deeply, and why should I not heed you?" Coyote could not see the spirit clearly. He appeared to be only a shadow. They started and went along over a plain. "Oh, there are many horses; it looks like a round-up," exclaimed the ghost.

"Yes," replied Coyote, though he really saw none, "yes, there are many horses."

They had arrived now near the place of the dead. The ghost knew that Coyote could see nothing but he said, "Oh look, such quantities of service berries! Let us pick some to eat. Now when you see me reach up you too will reach up and when I bend the limb down you too will pull your hands down." — "Yes," Coyote said to him, "so be it, thus I will do." The ghost reached up and bent the branch down and Coyote did the same. Although he could see no berries he imitated the ghost in putting his hand to and from his mouth in the manner of eating. Thus they picked and ate berries. Coyote watched him carefully and imitated every action. When the ghost would put his hand into his mouth Coyote would do the same. "Such good service berries these are," commented the ghost. "Yes, friend, it is good that we have found them," agreed Coyote. "Now let us go." And they went on.

"We are about to arrive," the ghost told him. "There is a long, very, very long lodge. Your wife is in there somewhere. Just wait and let me ask someone." In a little while the ghost returned and said to Coyote, "Yes, they have told me where your wife is. We are coming to a door through which we will enter. You will do in every way exactly what you see me do. I will take hold of the door flap, raise it up, and bending low, will enter. Then you too will take hold of the doorflap and do the same." They proceeded now in this manner to enter.

It happened that Coyote's wife was sitting right near the entrance. The ghost said to Coyote, "Sit here beside your wife." They both sat. The ghost added, "Your wife is now going to prepare food for us." Coyote could see nothing, except that he was sitting there on an open prairie where nothing was in sight; yet he could feel the presence of the shadow. "Now she has prepared our food. Let us eat." The ghost reached down and then brought his hand to his mouth. Coyote could see nothing but the prairie dust. They ate. Coyote imitated all the movements of his companion. When they had finished and the woman had apparently put the food away, the ghost said to Coyote, "You stay here. I must go around to see some people."

He went out but returned soon. "Here we have conditions different from those you have in the land of the living. When it gets dark here it has dawned in your land and when it dawns for us it is growing dark for you." And now it began to grow dark and Coyote seemed to hear people whispering, talking in faint tones, all around him. Then darkness set in. Oh, Coyote saw many fires in a long-house. He saw that he was in a very, very large lodge and there were many fires burning. He saw the various people. They seemed to have shadow-like forms but he was able to recognize different persons. He saw his wife sitting by his side.

He was overjoyed, and he joyfully greeted all his old friends who had died long ago. How happy he was! He would march down the aisles between the fires, going here and there, and talk with the people. He did this through-out the night. Now he could see the doorway through which he and his friend had entered. At last it began to dawn and his friend came to him and said, "Coyote, our night is falling and in a little while you will not see us. But you must stay right here. Do not go anywhere at all. Stay right here and then in the evening you will see all these people again." – "Yes, friend. Where could I possibly go? I will spend the day here."

The dawn came and Coyote found himself alone sitting there in the middle of a prairie. He spent the day there, just dying from the heat, parch-ing from the heat, thirsting from the heat. Coyote stayed here several days. He would suffer through the day, but always at night he would make merry in the great lodge.

One day his ghost friend came to him and said, "Tomorrow you will go home. You will take your wife with you." – "Yes, friend, but I like it here so much, I am having a good time and I should like to remain here." – "Yes," the ghost replied; "nevertheless you will go tomorrow, and you must guard against your inclination to do foolish things. Do not yield to any queer no-tions. I will advise you now what you are to do. There are five mountains. You will travel for five days. Your wife will be with you but you must never, never touch her. Do not let any strange impulses possess you. You may talk to her but never touch her. Only after you have crossed and descended from the fifth mountain you may do whatever you like." – "Yes, friend," replied Coyote.

When dawn came again Coyote and his wife started. At first it seemed to him as if he were going alone, yet he was dimly aware of his wife's pres-ence as she walked along behind. They crossed one mountain, and, now, Coyote could feel more definitely the presence of his wife; like a shadow she seemed. They went on and crossed the second mountain. They camped at night at the foot of each mountain. They had a little conical lodge which they would set up each time. Coyote's wife would sit on one side of the fire and he on the other. Her form appeared clearer and clearer.

The death spirit, who had sent them, now began to count the days and to figure the distance Coyote and his wife had covered. "I hope that he will do everything right and take his wife through to the world beyond," he kept saying to himself.

Here Coyote and his wife were spending their last night, their fourth camping, and on the morrow she would again assume fully the character of a living person. They were camping for the last time and Coyote could see her very clearly as if she were a real person who sat opposite him. He could see her face and body very clearly, but only looked and dared not touch her.

But suddenly a joyous impulse seized him; the joy of having his wife again overwhelmed him. He jumped to his feet, and rushed over to embrace her. His wife cried out, "Stop! Stop! Coyote! Do not touch me. Stop!" Her warning had no effect. Coyote rushed over to his wife and just as he touched her body she vanished. She disappeared—returned to the shadow-land.

When the death-spirit learned of Coyote's folly he became deeply angry. "You inveterate doer of this kind of thing! I told you not to do anything foolish. You, Coyote, were about to establish the practice of returning from death. Only a short time away the human race is coming, but you have spoiled everything and established for them death as it is."

Here Coyote wept and wept. He decided, "Tomorrow I shall return to see them again." He started back the following morning and as he went along he began to recognize the places where he and his spirit friend had passed before. He found the place where the ghost had seen the herd of horses, and now he began to do the same things they had done on their way to the shadow-land. "Oh, look at the horses; it looks like a round-up." He went on until he came to the place where the ghost had found the service berries. "Oh, such choice service berries! Let us pick and eat some." He went through the motions of picking and eating berries.

He went on and finally came to the place where the lodge had stood. He said to himself, "Now when I take hold of the door flap and raise it up you must do the same." Coyote remembered all the little things his friend had done. He saw the spot where he had sat before. He went there, sat down, and said, "Now, your wife has brought us food. Let us eat." He went through the motions of eating again. Darkness fell, and now Coyote listened for the voices, and he looked all around, he looked here and there, but nothing appeared. Coyote sat there in the middle of the prairie. He sat there all night but the lodge didn't appear again nor did the ghost ever return to him.[5]

More than most of the other narratives in *Nez Percé Texts,* "Coyote and the Shadow People" is intelligible without extensive ethnographic commentary, but it is helpful to know that the hero, Coyote, *itsayáya,* is usually a wily but reckless, self-seeking Trickster and adventurer in Nez Percé myths, much given to opportunistic deceptions (often for sex) that usually backfire outrageously. His classical mythic name in this role, according to Phinney, is *nasáwaylu.*[6] But like the Trickster in other Western Indian mythologies, Coyote is also the Nez Percé "transformer," the Myth Age personage who "travels about" transforming the unfinished world and its inhabitants and setting precedents (for better and for worse) that create reality as the latter-day Indians knew it. So, in this Orphic story, the awesome mythic powers in Coyote's complex role are emphasized, and to some extent he is made to seem capable of living up to these powers, as in his sustained grief for his wife and his persistence in seeking her: but the narrator clearly reminds us of Coyote's reputation as a Trickster, *nasáwaylu,* in the spirit guide's repeated warnings against doing "foolish things" and of course in his denunciation of Coyote near the end.

The mysterious "lodge of shadows" where Coyote finds his wife presumably had its real-life counterpart in the long pole-and-mat structures of the Nez Percés, pitched like tipis side by side with a continuous ridgepole; such a lodge, over one hundred feet long, was erected to house the death-feast of the great Nez Percé leader Joseph at Nespelem, Washington, in 1904.[7] Conceptually, the lodge reflects a widespread Western Indian view of the afterlife as a remote condition of the spirit in which the basic circumstances of earthly life are inverted: the night of the living is the daytime of the dead and vice versa, what is tangible to them is intangible to us (and the reverse), and so on. A morally neutral location—there is no alternative destination for the sinful—the Indian spirit-place seems to be at best a kind of eschatological afterthought, a "lodge of shadows" indeed where the surviving spirits exist not unpleasantly but without the raw immediacy and sweetness of mortal life. Early missionaries amongst the Nez Percés and other Great Plateau tribes were baffled by this conception of the essential goodness of earthly life set off by contrast with images of a shadowy, static afterlife; one of them, the Catholic Father Blanchet, complained that his native subjects "were surprised and provoked when I explained to them the blessedness of heaven; they appeared to like better the sojourn on this earth than to go away to enjoy celestial bliss."[8]

The narrative and dramatic strategies of "Coyote and the Shadow People" are conventional in native terms, and typical of Western Indian literature; and yet they seem, as they combine in this story, to achieve an imaginative power that is remarkable. In common with most Orphic stories, Indian and otherwise, the structure is highly symmetrical, details from before Coyote's arrival at the lodge corresponding to those coming afterward— a Journey In, and a Journey Out. Thus, the death of his wife, his mourning, and the initial appearance of the spirit guide are balanced by the final loss of his wife, his second mourning, and the final appearance of the spirit guide; his initial ritualized journey to the "lodge of shadows" is paralleled by the ritual stages of his journey back with his wife. In this symmetrical structure, only two main events are singular, set off by themselves—his joyful reunion with his dead wife, and his solitary second journey to the lodge—and the special significance of their being isolated as single actions we will see in a moment.

Of all the narrative strategies employed in Indian myth, *foreshadowing* appears most frequently, and with the widest latitude of effects. This has everything to do, of course, with the fact that the stories were well-known in outline to tribal audiences; with the outcome of a given story foreknown, the recitalist had a built-in condition of dramatic irony to exploit.[9] In the case of a story like "Coyote and the Shadow People," the ironic foreshadowing carries over beyond what only a Nez Percé listener would have recognized: we *all* know, after all, with varying degrees of conviction, that death is irrevocable, and final. Thus in a sense everything Coyote does in his quest foreshadows his failure, both for himself and his wife and for the great precedent of returning from death that he (as the death spirit's unknowing instrument) might establish. And yet, true to its genre (and to human nature), the story does set our unresigned human imaginations against our mortal knowledge of death's finality. We lend Coyote our dreams.

Specific prefigurements occur at every turn. There is the spirit guide's initial stern demand that Coyote—of all people, the Nez Percé Trickster!—must follow his instructions exactly, unquestioningly. The strange ritual en route involving invisible horses, a tent flap, and a meal are clearly *tests* of Coyote's imagination and will; he is rewarded for his unaccustomed self-control by seeing his wife and dead associates, but in the daytime, ominously, he loses all sight of them, and must "suffer through the day," "sitting there in the middle of a prairie"—the latter phrase a verbatim anticipation of the story's final narrative line. His complacent wish to remain in the lodge instead of returning home with his wife evidently contradicts the purposes of the spirit guide, both for Coyote and his wife and for the human race to come, and it too foreshadows the end. As does the spirit guide's unexplained injunction against touching his wife on the return trip: like all such taboos, it implies its own eventual tragic violation.

As for their journey back, the landscape through which Coyote and his wife travel is ritualized and programmatic, the five mountains serving as checkpoints for Coyote's tense progress: the brief appearance of the spirit guide at this point in the story, worrying about his protégé, notably heightens the tension. (Such intrusions are in fact uncommon in Western Indian narratives.) The fact that Coyote's wife grows day by day more tangible and real to him, of course, dramatizes the progressive heroic success of his quest to him—at the same time that it brings him, all too human, closer and closer to the forbidden but irresistible embrace, in a kind of vectoring of encouragement and temptation.

The climax, by the time it comes, is wholly foreshadowed; as usual, according to the *dramatic* premises of Indian narrative, its enactment is stark, tacit, "dramatic." We must imagine for ourselves the emotional reality evoked so economically by Coyote's impulsive gesture and his wife's cry—her one speech in the story.[10] That Coyote's loss of his wife, and indeed his unknowing forfeiture of the Orphic dream, should hinge on his inability to resist *touching* her rather than looking back at her, as in the Greek prototypes and many Indian versions, seems to me to be beautifully calculated to express the tragic paradox in Coyote's situation. He has been *seeing* his dead wife for some time now, but now that she appears to be fully tangible, seeing is not enough. To return to life again is to touch and be touched, ultimately in a sexual sense; Coyote would not "foolishly" violate the taboo and lose her if he did not love and desire her so much. To put the paradox another way, in terms of literary effect: if he *could* "take the long view" and restrain himself, the reality of his feelings for his wife would surely be suspect. The story asks its unblinking mythic question of us, Coyote's mortal inheritors: *Would we be able to do otherwise?* Well, at the level on which the story speaks to us as good citizens, obeyers of laws and keepers of taboos, I suppose we do answer, "Oh yes, we'd better do otherwise!" But to answer, on the heart's own level, "No, probably not," as I think we must, is to feel the peculiar mood of this myth—chastened, instructed, consoled. People die, we are reminded, and we cannot bring them back because they—and we—are in the nature of things imperfect, shortsighted, alive chiefly in the present moment; that is to say, we are mortal. The "truth" of all mythology is, finally, tautological.

Before taking up the story's final episode, I want to digress briefly on some parallels to this moment of climax and reversal in other native Orpheus stories from the Oregon Country, so as to at least point toward the imaginative diversity and psychological subtlety inherent in this kind of narrative. In the Wasco and Wishram Chinookan versions, as told along the Columbia River, Coyote and Eagle (a wise headman) both lose their wives; and after Eagle leads them on a highly complicated raid on the Lodge of Spirits and they are headed home again with a box containing the spirits of their wives and everyone else who has died, as well as samples of deciduous plants, Coyote begins to hear his wife's voice from within the box. Unable to wait until they reach home— there is no taboo as such—Coyote tricks Eagle into letting him carry the box, and seizes the first opportunity to unfasten the lid—whereupon all the spirits, including his wife, fly off in a great swarm, leaving only the plant samples in the box. Eagle denounces Coyote for his impatience, explaining that if they had gotten the box home intact, all people, as well as the trees and grasses, would die only for a season, and then return to life.[11]

In Melville Jacobs's great collection of Clackamas Chinook stories, there is an Orphic variant titled "Badger and Coyote Were Neighbors."[12] When Coyote's five children are killed trying to steal a wonderful ball from another village (as their ambitious and greedy father has urged them to do), he first attempts suicide by fire, water, and knife, and then, in the following spring, he undertakes to collect his children's bones and carry them home in such a magical way that they will be reanimated. Day by day he carries them homeward in his basket, very, very carefully; so slowly and deliberately does he move that on the fourth night he can look back and see his previous night's campfire. By now he can hear his children talking to one another. On the fifth and final day, however, an insect of some sort, "maybe a centipede," appears in Coyote's path, and taunts him by sniffing the air and declaring that "Coyote is carrying dead persons along! " At first Coyote controls himself, but at last loses his temper and chases after the insect—with the result that his nearly revived children are jostled and they die again, and with them all hope of bringing loved ones back, "just so," from death. It is left for Coyote, sadder and wiser, to invent the customs of mourning, whereby a mourner's grief will be limited in deference to the welfare of the tribe.

A few comparisons. In all three stories, Coyote takes his fatal hasty step in ignorance of the great human precedent he is throwing away: given his chronic self-centeredness and preoccupation with the moment, perhaps the point is being made that such grave knowledge would be irrelevant to him anyway, as a guide to action. He is inconstant and fallible: like us. The Wishram and Clackamas stories seem to have a wider etiological scope than the Nez Percé in that they couple the lost human precedent of returning from death with the achieved precedent of seasonal revivals among plants, as in the Persephone myth; the Nez Percé Coyote is denied even that Wordsworthian consolation. As for the moment of truth itself: you can take your pick from amongst three wonderfully vivid dramatizations, each having its own fix on human frailty and desire—the Wishram Coyote singling his wife's voice out of all the buzzing in the spirit-box, "like a great swarm of flies"; or the marvelous psychological projection of the Clackamas Coyote's internal doubts and impatience on a mocking insect in his path; or, again, the stark detail of the Nez Percé Coyote's *seeing* his wife's living body again, across the fire. Do we really want to call this kind of art "primitive"?

Now to carry on with the structure of the Nez Percé story. Before, we noticed that two of its events are structurally singular and unbalanced—Coyote's reunion with his wife, and his second quest for her, by himself. The reunion stands alone, of course, because the return to life and home it is to be an initial stage of, is doomed. As for Coyote's second quest, begun after the final meaning of his Orphic failure has been emphatically spelled out to him, so far as I know it is unique in North American native literature. In this surprising final episode, the narrative seems to move beyond the modus and logic of myth *per se,* assuming a status more like that of fiction—as if Coyote has now entered *our* kind of reality.

At the end of many Indian Orpheus stories, the failed quester *wants* to go back after his lost loved one, but will not or cannot oppose the precedent he has just established. In Phinney's other Orpheus story, for example, after Coyote has "looked back" and thus lost his chance to carry his daughter all the way back from death, he pleads, "Let me follow you back and I will bring you again"; but the offer is refused and after a little weeping, he wanders off.[13] But here, on some level of consciousness at least, Coyote actually does set out again, as if moving beyond the finalized terms of his own myth, as explained to him by the spirit guide. Now it is possible that this episode would have struck Nez Percé listeners as a kind of ironic analogue to the solitary and highly ritualized visionary quests on which all native religions in the Far West were founded—Coyote, having had genuine commerce with the spirit world and having violated its terms, can now only go through the motions, as if in a dream. Indeed, it may be that behind all the weird journeys and heroic ordeals in Nez Percé and other Western repertoires, there stands, ultimately, the cultural archetype of the spirit quest.[14]

But this is extracurricular speculation, and I think a more helpful literary parallel to the episode of Coyote's attempted return can be found in myths, from a variety of tribes, which dramatize the origin of death itself. Typically, a Myth Age person decrees that, according to some abstract philanthropical principle—the danger of overcrowding and famine, for example—people will have to die. Then the decreer in fact suffers the first mortal loss (often it is a child who dies) and, humanlike, pleads unavailingly with the Creator for a repeal or postponement of the new law. In the Blackfoot "Old Man" cycle, for instance, First Woman opts for universal human mortality for a compelling but highly abstract reason: "so people will be sorry for one another."[15] But when her son dies soon afterward, she rejects this wisdom and begs "Old Man," unsuccessfully, to change the Way. Like Coyote in his second return, First Woman appears to move beyond her mythic situation *per se* into the common tragic experience of mortality; she and Coyote both actively "suffer," as if in a fictive work, their own myths, as we do in real life who follow them.[16]

Where before Coyote is, as we say, "all too human" in wanting to touch his wife so ardently in a moment that he loses her forever, so here, in this post-Orphic sequel he is shown to be poignantly, definitively human in his confidence that his own unaided imagination and desire, supplemented by a little ceremonial knowledge, will suffice to carry him back to the lodge of the shadow people and his wife, despite the mythic precedent he has just set. His actions in retracing his steps and playing both himself and the spirit guide "just so" are at once heroic and ridiculous; here he becomes most fully integrated as himself, Coyote *itsayáya* and *nasáwaylu.* The end of his quest, with Coyote sitting alone "there in the middle of the prairie," has an affective resonance and finality beyond any other Orpheus story I know.

Wayilatpu's Nez Percé narrative gives us Coyote as an image

of human loss, mythically speaking the first in a long unbroken line of unresigned mourners who again and again wake up from their Orphic dreams into what Yeats called "the desolation of reality."[17] But it is a desolation for which, through the story, we have words and a human image.

The Origin of Eternal Death[18]

Coyote had a wife and two children, and so had Eagle. Both families lived together. Eagle's wife and children died, and a few days later Coyote experienced the same misfortune. As the latter wept, his companion said: "Do not mourn: that will not bring your wife back. Make ready your moccasins, and we will go somewhere." So the two prepared for a long journey, and set out westward.

After four days they were close to the ocean; on one side of a body of water they saw houses. Coyote called across, "Come with a boat!" "Never mind; stop calling," bade Eagle. He produced an elderberry stalk, made a flute, put the end into the water, and whistled. Soon they saw two persons come out of a house, walk to the water's edge, and enter a canoe. Said Eagle, "Do not look at those people when they land." The boat drew near, but a few yards from the shore it stopped, and Eagle told his friend to close his eyes. He then took Coyote by the arm and leaped to the boat. The two persons paddled back, and when they stopped a short distance from the other side Eagle again cautioned Coyote to close his eyes, and then leaped ashore with him.

They went to the village, where there were many houses, but no people were in sight. Everything was still as death. There was a very large underground house, into which they went. In it was found an old woman sitting with her face to the wall, and lying on the floor on the other side of the room was the moon. They sat down near the wall.

"Coyote," whispered Eagle, "watch that woman and see what she does when the sun goes down!" Just before the sun set they heard a voice outside calling: "Get up! Hurry! The sun is going down, and it will soon be night. Hurry, hurry!" Coyote and Eagle still sat in a corner of the chamber watching the old woman. People began to enter, many hundreds of them, men, women, and children. Coyote, as he watched, saw Eagle's wife and two daughters among them, and soon afterward his own family. When the room was filled, Nikshiámchásht, the old woman, cried, "Are all in?" Then she turned about, and from a squatting posture she jumped forward, then again and again, five times in all, until she alighted in a small pit beside the moon. This she raised and swallowed, and at once it was pitch dark. The people wandered about, hither and thither, crowding and jostling, unable to see. About daylight a voice from outside cried, "Nikshiámchásht, all get through!" The old woman then disgorged the moon, and laid it back in its place on the floor; all the people filed out, and the woman, Eagle, and Coyote were once more alone.

"Now, Coyote," said Eagle, "could you do that?" "Yes, I can do that," he said. They went out, and Coyote at Eagle's direction made a box of boards, as large as he could carry, and put into it leaves from every kind of tree and blades from every kind of grass. "Well," said Eagle, "if you are sure you remember just how she did this, let us go in and kill her." So they entered the house and killed her, and buried the body. Her dress they took off and put on Coyote, so that he looked just like her, and he sat down in her place. Eagle then told him to practise what he had seen, by turning around and jumping as the old woman had done. So Coyote turned about and jumped five times, but the last leap was a little short, yet he managed to slide into the hole. He put the moon into his mouth, but, try as he would, a thin edge still showed, and he covered it with his hands. Then he laid it back in its place and resumed his seat by the wall, waiting for sunset and the voice of the chief outside.

The day passed, the voice called, and the people entered. Coyote turned about and began to jump. Some thought there was something strange about the manner of jumping, but others said it was really the old woman. When he came to the last jump and slipped into the pit, many cried out that this was not the old woman, but Coyote quickly lifted the moon and put it into his mouth, covering the edge with his hands. When it was completely dark, Eagle placed the box in the doorway. Throughout the long night Coyote retained the moon in his mouth, until he was almost choking, but at last the voice of the chief was heard from the outside, and the dead began to file out. Every one walked into the box, and Eagle quickly threw the cover over and tied it. The sound was like that of a great swarm of flies. "Now, my brother, we are through," said Eagle. Coyote removed the dress and laid it down beside the moon, and Eagle threw the moon into the sky, where it remained. The two entered the canoe with the box, and paddled toward the east.

When they landed, Eagle carried the box. Near the end of the third night Coyote heard somebody talking; there seemed to be many voices. He awakened his companion, and said, "There are many people coming." "Do not worry," said Eagle; "it is all right." The following night Coyote heard the talking again, and, looking about, he discovered that the voices came from the box which Eagle had been carrying. He placed his ear against it, and after a while distinguished the voice of his wife. He smiled, and broke into laughter, but he said nothing to Eagle. At the end of the fifth night and the beginning of their last day of travelling, he said to his friend, "I will carry the box now; you have carried it a long way." "No," replied Eagle, "I will take it; I am strong." "Let me carry it," insisted the other; "suppose we come to where people live, and they should see the chief carrying the load. How would that look?" Still Eagle retained his hold on the box, but as they went along Coyote kept begging, and about noon, wearying of the subject, Eagle gave him the box. So Coyote had the load, and every time he heard the voice of his wife he would laugh. After a while he contrived to fall behind, and when Eagle was out of sight around a hill he began to open the box, in order to release his wife. But no sooner was the cover lifted than it was thrown back violently, and the dead people rushed out into the air with such force that Coyote was thrown to the ground. They quickly disappeared in the west. Eagle saw the cloud of dead people rising in the air, and came hurrying back. He found one man left there, a cripple who had been unable to rise; he threw him into the air, and the dead man floated away swiftly.

"You see what you have done, with your curiosity and haste!" said Eagle. "If we had brought these dead all the way back, people would not die forever, but only for a season, like these plants, whose leaves we have brought. Hereafter trees and grasses will die only in the winter, but in the spring they will be green again. So it would have been with the people." "Let us go back and catch them again," proposed Coyote; but Eagle objected: "They will not go to the same place, and we would not know how to find them; they will be where the moon is, up in the sky."

Badger and Coyote Were Neighbors[19]

Coyote and his five children lived there (at an undisclosed location), four males, one female. Badger was a neighbor there, he had five children, all males. Each day they (all ten children) would go here and there. They came back in the evening. And the next day they would go again. Now that is the way they were doing. They would go all over, they traveled about.

Now they reached a village, they stayed up above there, they looked down below at it, they saw where they (the villagers) were playing ball. And as they stayed there and watched, the people (of the village beneath) saw them now. They went to the place there where they played ball. Now they (the villagers) played. When they threw the ball it (that ball) was just like the sun. Now they stayed (above) there, they watched them playing. Sometimes it (the ball) would drop close by them. Now they quit (playing). Then they (the ten children who were watching) went back home, they went to their houses.

The next day then they did not go anywhere. All day long they chatted about that ball (and schemed about stealing it). They discussed it. Now their father Badger heard them. He said to his sons, "What is it that you are discussing?" So they told their father. "Yes," they said to him, "we got to a village, and they were playing ball. When the ball went it was just like the sun. We thought that we would go get it." Now then he said to his children, "What do you think (about talking this over with Coyote too)?" So then they said to Coyote, "What do you think?" He said, "My children should be the first ones (to run with the ball), if they bring the ball." Badger said, "No. My children should be the first ones to do it (run with the stolen ball)." Coyote said, "No. My children have long bodies, their legs are long. They can **run** (faster than your children). Your children have short legs." So then he replied to him (to Coyote), "Very well then."

Now the next day they got ready, and they went. They reached there. At that place one of them (the oldest son of Coyote) went immediately to the spot where the ball might drop. He covered (buried) himself at that place (on the playing field). Then another (the next oldest son) buried himself farther on, and another one (the third in age) still farther away. All four (sons of Coyote) covered themselves (with soil on the field). The last one farther on at the end (was) their younger sister. Now the (five) children of Badger merely remained (on the hill above the field), they watched.

Soon afterwards then the people (of that village) came to there, they came to play ball. Now they threw the ball to where it fell close by him (Coyote's oldest son). He seized it. They looked for it, they said, (because they knew that) "Coyote's son is hiding it!" He let it go, and they took it, and they played more. Now it dropped close by him there once again. So then he took it, and he ran. The people turned and looked, they saw him running, he was taking the ball. Now they ran in pursuit, they got close to him, he got close to his younger brother (the second in age), he threw the ball to him. He said to him, "We are dying (going to be killed) because of the ball. Give a large chunk of it to our father." (His pursuers now caught up to and killed him.) Then the other (the second) one took it, and he ran too. The people pursued him, he got close to his young brother (Coyote's third son). Now they seized him (the second son), and he threw it to his younger brother. They killed all four of them. Now only their younger sister held the ball, she ran, she ran and ran, she left them quite a distance (behind because she was the fastest runner of them all). She got close to the Badgers. Now as they (the villagers who pursued) seized her she threw the ball to them (to the five Badger children), she said to them, "Give the biggest portion to our father (to Coyote). We have died because of the ball."

The Badgers took the ball. He (the first and oldest Badger child) dropped it when he picked it up. Another (the next to the oldest) took it, he also dropped it when he picked it up. They (the pursuers) got to there, and the people stood there (watching the Badger children fumbling the ball). They said, they told them, "So those are the ones who would be taking away the ball!" They laughed at them (at the seemingly clumsy Badger children). They said, "Let it be a little later before we kill them!" Soon now they (the Badgers) kicked at the ground, and wind blew (and) dust (and) darkness stood there. Dust covered (everything), and the wind blew. Now the Badgers ran, they ran away with the ball. And those people pursued them. They got tired, they got thirsty (from wind and dust), they (the pursuers) turned back to their home.

On the other hand those others (the Badgers) lay down (because of exhaustion) right there when they had gotten close (to their own home). And there they sat (and rested). Now they hallooed, they said to their father, "Badger! we left your children far back there!" Now they hallooed again, they went and told Coyote, "Back yonder we left your children." That is the way they did to them (they first deceived Badger and Coyote). Now Badger went outside, he said to his children, "Now really why did you do like that? You have been teasing and paining him (Coyote)." Then they (the Badger children) went downhill (and entered the village), it was only Badger's children (who returned). They brought the ball with them.

Now Coyote tried in vain to drown himself. He did not die. Then he built a fire, he made a big fire, he leaped into it there. He did not burn, he did not die. He took a rope, he tied it, he tied it on his throat, he pulled himself up, once more he did not die. He took a knife, he cut his throat, (again) he did not die. He did every sort of thing that he intended for killing himself. He gave up. I do not know how many days he was doing like that (trying one or another means of committing suicide). Now he quit it, and he merely wept all the day long. (After a while) he gave that up (too).

Then Badger said to his children, "He has quit (mourning) now. So then cut up the ball for him. Give him half." And they did that for him, they gave him half. He took it, and he went here and there at the place where his children used to play. There he now mashed (into many pieces) that ball, at the place where they used to play. That was where he took it, he mashed it up, the ball was entirely gone (now).

Then they continued to live there, and Coyote was all alone. Now he went to work, he made a loose big pack basket. Then it was getting to be springtime, and when the leaves were coming out, now he got ready, and he went to the place there where they had killed his children. He got to the (grave of the) first one (his oldest son). He picked ferns, he lined his pack basket with them. He got to the place where they had killed the first of his sons, he collected his bones, he put them into it (into the basket), he laid them in it neatly. Then he got more ferns, he picked the leaves, he covered (the bones of) his son. Now he went a little farther, and he again got to bones (of his second son). Then he also put them into it (into the basket), and that is the way he did again. He collected the bones of all five of his children.

Now he went on, he proceeded very very slowly, he went only a short distance. Then he camped overnight. The next day he proceeded again, also very slowly like that. On the fifth day, then he heard them (talking to one another in the basket). They said, "You are lying upon me. Move a little." Then he went along all the more slowly. Now he kept going, he went just a short distance, and then he picked more leaves, he covered it all (with utmost care and constant replenishing with fresh leaves). And that is the way he did as he went along.

She (perhaps a centipede) would run across his path, she would say to him, "Sniff sniff sniff! (because of the bad odor of decaying flesh) Coyote is taking dead persons along!" He paid no heed to her. Now she ran repeatedly and all the more in front of him, again she would speak like that to him, "Sniff! Coyote is carrying dead persons along!" He laid his basket down very very slowly (with utmost care), he got a stick, he ran after her. I do not know where she went and hid.

Then he packed his carrying basket on his back again, and now he went very very slowly, and he heard his children. Now they were chatting, they were saying, "Move around slowly and carefully! we are making our father tired." Then he was glad, and he went along even more slowly and cautiously. (He walked so very slowly that) he saw his (previous night's) campfire, and then he again camped overnight.

He went on again the next morning, and then that thing (the bug) ran back and forth across his path right there by his feet. Now he became angry. He placed his basket down, and again he chased it. I do not know where it hid.

On the fifth day then he heard them laughing. So he went along even more painstakingly. Now that thing went still more back and forth in front of him by his feet. He forgot (in his great irritation and tension), he (much too abruptly) loosened and let go his pack basket. "Oh oh oh" his children sounded (and at once died from the shock of the sudden movement of the basket). All done, he finished, and he again put back his basket on himself. When he went along now he did not hear them talking at all. He went along then. They were dead now when he uncovered his basket. Only bones were inside it. He reached his house. The following day then they buried them. He finished (with that effort). He wept for five days.

Then he said, "Indeed I myself did like that (and lost my children because of my doing). The people (who will populate this country) are coming and close by now. Only in that one manner shall it be, when persons die. In that one way had I brought my children back, then the people would be like that (in later eras). When they died in summertime wintertime or toward springtime, after the leaves (came on the trees) they (all the dead) would have come back to life, and such persons would have revived on the fifth day (following a ritual like the one I attempted). But now his (any mourner's) sorrow departs from him after ten days (of formal mourning). Then he can go to anywhere where something (entertaining) is happening or they are gambling (and) he may (then shed his mourning and) watch on at it."

Notes

1. A version of this essay was read at the 1976 meeting of the Rocky Mountain Modern Language Association, in Santa Fe, New Mexico, October 1976. The essay originally appeared in *Western American Literature* 13, no. 2 (August 1978). On the Orpheus theme see Åke Hultkrantz's very full study, *The North American Indian Orpheus Tradition,* Ethnological Museum of Sweden Monograph Series, no. 2 (Stockholm, 1957); oddly enough, Hultkrantz ignores our text. Also see Anne Gayton, "The Orpheus Myth in North America," *Journal of American Folklore* 48 (July-September 1935): 263-93. Gayton's study apparently came out too early for her to consider Phinney's collection.

2. Archie Phinney, *Nez Percé Texts,* Columbia University Contributions to Anthropology, vol. 25 (New York: Columbia University Press, 1934), p. vii.

3. MS letter, dated 20 November 1929, in the collection of the American Philosophical Society Library, Philadelphia, and printed here with the permission of the Society.

4. Phinney, *Nez Percé Texts,* p. ix.

5. Phinney, *Nez Percé Texts,* pp. 282-85. Phinney presents the story as a "second version" of another Orpheus story, "Coyote the Interloper" (pp. 268-81), but in fact the two are radically different. For reasons unknown to me Phinney does not give the Nez Percé language text for "Coyote and the Shadow People," as he does for the rest of his stories. The English text is reprinted, with notes, in my anthology of Indian literature from the Oregon Country, *Coyote Was Going There* (Seattle: University of Washington Press, 1977).

6. In Phinney's collection, for example, see "Coyote Causes His Son to Be Lost," "Bat and Coyote," and "Bears and Coyote," in which (p. 480) a Bear says to Coyote, "Vile you are, Coyote" (*nasáwaylu*).

7. For an account of the event, and photographs of the lodge, see Edward S. Curtis, *The North American Indian,* vol. 8 (Norwood, Mass.: The Plimpton Press, 1911), p. 40. The appearance of the lodge and the reference to the "conical lodge" (tipi) that Coyote and his wife use en route home, in connection with the references to horses and a roundup, suggest that the story as we have it dates from not before the middle of the eighteenth century, after the appearance of horses and horseback encounters with Plains culture.

8. Father Blanchet in *Notices and Voyages of the Famous Quebec Mission to the Pacific Northwest,* ed. and trans. Carl Landerholm (Portland: Champoey Press, 1956), p. 68.

9. I discuss the use and effects of foreshadowing in "The Wife Who Goes Out like a Man, Comes Back as a Hero," *PMLA* 92, no. 1 (January 1977): 9-18.

10. It is a measure of this story's pervasive seriousness that, whereas in other of Phinney's texts Coyote is variously—and comically—married to wives identified as Mouse (evidently his favorite), "Lady Bullfrog," White Swan, and "flying people," here the wife has no animal or typological identity; she is only "Coyote's wife," and is recognized only by him and by the spirit guide.

11. The Wishram story is in Curtis, *The North American Indian*, 8: 127-29. Another Wishram version is in Edward Sapir, *Wishram Texts*, Publications of the American Ethnological Society, vol. 2 (Leyden, N.J.: E. J. Brill, 1909), pp. 107-17; the same collection contains a Wasco version transcribed by Jeremiah Curtin (pp. 127-29).

12. Text and commentary are given in Jacobs's pioneering study, *The Content and Style of an Oral Literature* (Seattle: University of Washington Press, 1959), pp. 27-36.

13. Phinney, *Nez Percé Texts*, p. 282.

14. For ethnographic commentary see Herbert Spinden, *The Nez Percé Indians, Memoirs of the American Anthropological Association,* vol. 2, pt. 3 (1908); and Curtis, *The North American Indian*, 8: 52-76.

15. George Bird Grinnell, *Blackfoot Lodge Tales* (1892; rpt. Lincoln: University of Nebraska Press, 1962), p. 139. For a view of Tricksters as creators of death in some Indian myths, see M. L. Ricketts's essay, "The North American Indian Trickster," *History of Religions* 5 (1966): 327-50.

16. In "Serial Order in Nez Percé Myths," *Journal of American Folklore* 86 (1971): 104-17, Brian Stross examines "myth initials" and "myth finals" —the opening and closing expressions of the narratives—in relation to other kinds of serial order in them, and finds two kinds of myth finals: "Either the audience leaves the scene of action while the actor or actors remain in a state of relative inaction . . . or else the actor or actors leave the scene of action without a corresponding shift of scene by the narrator." In the second form of ending "the audience is transported from the world of myth to the world of reality by means of an explanatory connection between the two" (p. 108). In the case of "Coyote and the Shadow People," Coyote's last episode seems to conclude with Stross's first kind of myth final, and yet in *effect*— our sense of movement from mythic to fictive representation of reality—it seems to correspond to his second kind, albeit without formulaic expression or "explanatory connection." In fact those elements have already appeared at what would be the conventional ending of the story, before Coyote's last quest, when the death spirit tells him, "Only a short time away the human race is coming, but you have spoiled everything and established for them death as it is."

17. William Butler Yeats, "Meru," *The Collected Poems of William Butler Yeats* (New York: Macmillan and Co., 1950), p. 333.

18. "The Origin of Eternal Death" (Wishram) from vol. 8, *The North*

American Indian, by Edward S. Curtis (Norwood, Mass.: The Plimpton Press, 1911). Informant unknown, transcription and translation probably by W. E. Myers.

19. Melville Jacobs, *The Content and Style of an Oral Literature* (New York: Wenner-Gren Foundation, 1959), pp. 27-29. Informant: Mrs. Victoria Howard.

DENNIS TEDLOCK

The Spoken Word
and the Work of Interpretation
in American Indian Religion

Our text for this morning comes from the Aashiwi, as they call themselves, or from the Zuni Indians. They live in a town in west-central New Mexico and are now twice as numerous as they were when the Spanish first counted them in 1540. Their language is *shiwi'ma*,[1] one of the 150 languages spoken by the various indigenous peoples of the United States.

The name of the text is *chimiky'ana'kowa*. Literally translated, that means "that which was the beginning." It *is* the beginning, or "that which *was* the beginning." These words were made by what happened at the beginning, and to tell these words is to happen the beginning again. *Chimiky'ana'kowa*.

I speak of a *text*, even though the Zunis do not have a *manuscript* of the beginning. But there is a way of fixing *words* without making visible *marks*. As with alphabetical writing, this fixing is done by a *radical simplification* of ordinary talk. Ordinary talk not only has words in it, in the sense of strings of consonants and vowels, but it has patterns of stress, of emphasis, of pitch, of tone, of pauses or stops that can move somewhat independently of the sheer words and make the "same" words mean quite different things, or even the opposite of what they started out to mean.[2] To *fix a text* without making *visible marks* is to bring *stress* and *pitch* and *pause* into a fixed relationship with the *words*. The Zunis call this *ana k'eyato'u*, "raising it right up," and we would call it chant. In Zuni chant, a strong stress and a high, gliding pitch come into concert on the last syllable of each phrase, or sometimes at the end of a single important word, and are immediately followed by a deliberate silence. All other, weaker stresses occurring between two pauses are equal, and all lower pitches are resolved into a monotone.[3] The number of syllables between two pauses varies from around six or seven to twenty or more. This variation has the effect of giving emphasis to the shortest lines, but this is an emphasis *fixed* in the *text* rather than being left to the voice of an individual speaker on a particular occasion. It all sounds something like this (monotone chant, with strong stress and a quick rise on each line—final syllable):

> Nomilhte ho'n chimiky'anapkya teya
> awiten tehwula
> annohsiyan tehwula
> ho'na liilha aateyaye . . .

> Now in truth our beginning is:
> the fourth inner world
> the soot inner world
> is where we live . . .[4]

The words, or rather the word, of the *chimiky'ana'kowa,* "that which was the beginning," is fixed in a text called *Kyaklo 'an penanne,* the Word of Kyaklo.[5] Kyaklo is a person, a Zuni, who witnessed some of the events of the beginning. He comes once each four or eight years to give his word. He is a stubborn, cranky cripple who must be carried everywhere he goes by the ten clowns who accompany him, and he always demands that the smallest one do it. He always comes into town by the same path, the same path he has followed since the beginning. There is a new subdivision whose streets do not follow his path, so he must be carried through people's yards. There is a house that sits in his path, so he must be carried up over the roof and down the other side. When they come to the river, just before entering the old part of town, he insists that the clowns wade through the ice and mud of the river rather than taking the bridge. He wears the finest clothes, but they always manage to drop him in the river. Kyaklo's face is bordered by the rainbow and the milky way, and rain falls from his eyes and mouth. All he does, besides chanting, is to call out his own name: "Kyaklo Kyaklo Kyaklo Kyaklo." The people who want to hear his word assemble in six different ceremonial chambers, or kivas.[6] He carries a duck in his right hand, and if anyone falls asleep while he talks, he hits them with the duck's bill. He goes from one building to the next, still chanting even while being carried through the streets; no one person hears the whole word on one occasion, except for the clowns who carry him. On top of that, he uses a lot of arcane and esoteric vocabulary, so that those who are not well-versed in such matters have difficulty in following. Worse than that, he chants rather fast and his words are muffled by his mask. To wear Kyaklo's mask, a person must devote his whole life, for one year, to studying for the part.

So there is our text. Like a cleanly alphabetic text, it consists of a sheer string of words. Kyaklo always pronounces the same words in the same way; it is always Kyaklo chanting, not a particular wearer of the mask. There are no shifts of stress or pitch or pause to find a new meaning, to say nothing of a search for different *words*. Such is the nature of what we call "authoritative texts": they go on saying exactly the same thing, over and over, forever. Any way you look at it, Kyaklo is authoritative text personified.

Now, the *interpretation* of the *chimiky'ana'kowa,* "that which was the beginning," is another matter. The story does not end with Kyaklo. There are fourteen priesthoods at Zuni, charged with meditation on the weather and with divination, and each of them has an interpretation of the beginning.[7] There are thirteen medicine societies, charged with curing, and each of them has an interpretation. And in every Zuni household there is at least one parent or grandparent who knows how to interpret the beginning. I say "interpretation" partly because we are no longer speaking of absolutely fixed texts. The stresses, pitches, pauses, and also the *sheer words,* are different from one interpreter to the next, and even from one occasion to the next, according to the place and time, according to who is in the audience, according to what they do or do not already know, according to what questions they may have asked. Even according to what may happen, outside the events of the narrative itself, during this particular telling.[8] Or the interpreter may suddenly realize something or understand something for the first time on this particular occasion. The teller is not merely repeating memorized words, nor is he or she merely giving a dramatic "oral interpretation" or "concert reading" of a fixed script. We are in the presence of a *performing art*, all right, but we are getting the *criticism* at the same time and from the same person. The interpreter does not merely play the parts, but is the narrator and commentator as well. What we are hearing is the *hermeneutics* of the text of Kyaklo. At times we may hear direct quotations from that text, but they are embedded in a hermeneutics.

Now, our own phenomenologists and structuralists also quote their texts, removing words from context and even daring to insert their own *italics*: "italics mine." But there is a difference here: the interpreter of that which was the beginning must keep the *story* going. And in this process, the storyteller-interpreter does not merely quote or paraphrase the text but may even *improve* upon it, describe a scene which it does not describe, or answer a question which it does not answer.

The Word of Kyaklo, taken by itself, is a sacred object, a relic. It is not a visible or tangible object, but it is an object nevertheless. What we hear from our interpreter is simultaneously something new *and* a comment on that relic, both a restoration and a further possibility. I emphasize this point because ethnologists, down to the present day, have hankered after the sacred object itself, whenever they could get their hands on it, while devaluing what I am here calling "interpretations." Dell Hymes falls into this pattern when he makes a distinction between what he calls "a *telling about* the story" and "a *doing of* the story" (italics mine).[9] He suggests that we need to gather up the "true performances" from our collections of North American narratives, sorting these out from the mere "tellings," or "reportings," which exist in these same collections. What is stark about this position is that it leaves the "telling about" the story, including commentary and interpretation, entirely up to the ethnologist, while the proper business of the native is limited to the "doing of" the story. This is close to the position of the French structuralists, who limit the native to a narrative or "diachronic" function and concede exclusive rights to the analytic or "synchronic" function to themselves. In effect, the collected texts are treated as if they were raw products, to which value is then added by manufacture.

For the Zuni storyteller-interpreter, the relationship between text and interpretation is a dialectical one: he or she both respects the text and revises it. But for the ethnologist, that relationship is a dualistic opposition. In the end, the text remains the text, still there in the archives and still waiting to be brought to light; the analysis remains the analysis, bearing no resemblance *to* the text and learning nothing *from* the text, and the analyst even takes professional pride in that fact.

The interpretation of the Kyaklo text that concerns us here was given by a man named Andrew Peynetsa, then sixty-two years old, at his farmhouse in the evening.[10] Checking my notes, I find that he gave the first part of this narrative thirteen years ago last Sunday and finished it thirteen years ago today, on March 29, 1965. He was talking to his wife, one of his sons, his brother, and me. I, of course, had a tape recorder, and my translation from the Zuni follows not only the original words but also the original loudnesses, softnesses, tones, and silences.

Andrew, as a boy, had heard the entire Word of Kyaklo. He and a cousin had been pestering their grandfather to tell a tale, the kind of story the Zunis tell for entertainment. Their grandfather was a cranky old man who didn't really know any tales, but one night he finally consented to tell them something. It turned out to be the Word of Kyaklo. He kept them awake all night, hitting them with a stick whenever they nodded. At dawn he sent them out to do their chores. The next night he resumed his talk, going on all night again. And so on for another night and another, finishing at dawn on the fourth day.

The Zuni beginning does not begin with a first cause; it does not derive an infinite chain of dualisms from a first dualism that in turn springs from original absolute oneness. When the story opens, the earth is already here, the *awitelin tsitta,* literally the "four-chambered mother." There are four more worlds under this one, darker and darker. In this room we're on the third floor, so the bottommost world beneath this one would be a secret basement below the actual basement of this building.[11] Only the Sun Father is up here in this world. Four stories beneath in the Soot Room, in total darkness, are the people. The problem is not to create human beings, but that they should be up here in this world, making prayers and offerings to the Sun Father and receiving his daylight, his life. The people down in the fourth room beneath are only *moss people*; they have webbed feet, webbed hands, tails of moss; they are slimy. They do not know what fire is, or lightning, or daylight, or even dawn.

In the Word of Kyaklo and in all previously recorded interpretations, the three rooms between this world and the Soot

Room are apparently vacant.[12] This is where Andrew's interpretation introduces one of its elaborations or improvements:[13]

> At the beginning
> when the earth was still soft
> the first people came out
> the ones who had been living in the first room beneath.
> When they came out they made their villages
> they made their houses a——ll around the land.

So the first people out were not ourselves, as in the other versions, but people who were living in the first room beneath this one. But the Sun Father was displeased because "they did not think of anything," they did not give prayers and offerings. When the people in the second room came out, their sulphurous smell, their ozone smell killed all the first ones. They in turn did not think of anything. The people from the third room beneath came out, and their sulphurous smell killed the second people, and they, too, did not think of anything.

Now, the idea that three unsuccessful approximations of human beings preceded ourselves is a common one among Meso-american peoples, far to the south of the Zunis. But it is not our concern here to pretend to "explain" the source, the origin of this part of the present narrative. The point is that Kyaklo leaves three rooms vacant, and our interpreter fills them. This may be something "new," or it may even be a restoration of something that Kyaklo forgot. Whatever the case, these first three peoples live and die in a storyteller's *interpretation* and not in the chanter's *text*. They are *not* in the "book."

As we heard before, these previous people "made their villages a——ll around the land." Our interpreter stops for a moment to comment on this:

> Their ruins are all around the land as you can see.
> Around the mountains where there is no water today, you
>   could get water just by pulling up a clump of grass
> because the earth was soft.
> This is the way they lived, there at the beginning.

Not only is this a departure from the official text; it is a departure from the "doing of" the story, and it changes over from third person narrative to direct address: "as *you* can see." Interpretation, here in the form of a small lecture, in the very *midst* of the *text.* It happens again just a few lines later, as the narrator leads us toward the moment when the twin sons of the Sun Father come into existence. It had been raining all night:

> Where there were waterfalls
> the water made foam.
> Well, you know how water can make foam
> certainly
> it can make foam
>
> certainly
> that water
> made suds.
> It was there
> where the suds were made
> that the two Bow Priests
> sprouted.
> There the two Ahayuuta
> received life.
> Their father brought them to life:
> they came out of the suds.

And in another place, having told an episode in which Nepayatamu, the patron of the Clown Society, brings the Molaawe, or corn deities, back into the town after a famine, our interpreter comments:

> When the Molaawe enter today
> the same procedure is followed:
> Nepayatamu
> does not speak
> when he enters
> and the priests are completely quiet inside, well you
> have seen this yourself, at the kiva.

Such passages as these raise questions about the relationship of text to world. I mean "world" in the sense that Paul Ricoeur does when he says that the task of hermeneutics is to reveal the "destination of discourse as projecting a world," or when he says that "for me, the world is the ensemble of references opened up by every kind of text."[14] But when the ruins are all around the land, as *you* can see; when *you* know how water can make foam, can make suds; when *you* have seen Nepayatamu and the Molaawe yourself, at the kiva, I don't know whether the text is opening up the world, or the world is opening up the text. This problem is written larger in the narrative as a whole. The world was *already there*; we human beings, or "daylight people" as the Zunis call us, were already there; and, as the narrative details, there were already priesthoods and even a whole village down there in the Soot Room, and the priesthoods were in possession of the seeds of every kind of plant that would grow up here in this world. Still, it is true, we were in the dark, and the world up here on this layer, even if it already existed, had not yet been revealed to us. The Sun Father gave his twin sons the *word* that we were to come out into the daylight, and they brought that *word* down to the priests. The priests responded by setting themselves the very lengthy project of getting us out into the daylight. It looks as though the discourse of the Sun Father had, to paraphrase Ricoeur, projected a world for us. Or, if we follow Ricoeur's recent abandonment of the phenomenological concern with the author's intentions, the Word itself projects a world for us. But "project": that seems like the disembodied ghost of the author's intention, the will of God working itself out in the creation of the world. There is something too inevitable about it all. The word in the Zuni beginning, the word brought by the twin sons of the Sun Father, is *pewiyulhahna,* a word that is *yulhahna*: *lha-* means important, or even *too* important, *too* much, but the *-hna* on the end makes that negative and the *yu-* on the front puts the word in the indeterminative: *yulhahna,* "sort of not too important," or the word is of "indeterminate importance." It is a word of *some* importance, but perhaps not *too* much.

The Kyaklo text and the available priestly interpretations hint at a general theme of indeterminacy that goes beyond terminological questions, but Andrew's interpretation develops that theme fully. First of all, when the people from the first room emerge into this world, he does not even mention that the Sun Father played any role. When it comes to the second people, the Sun Father simply remarks, "Well, perhaps if the ones who live in the second room come out, it will be good." For the third people, the narrator says, "Those who lived in the third room beneath were summoned"; if it was the Sun Father who summoned them, this is only implicit, but at least we have a glimpse of a will here. Now, we may think, the next stage will be to put the Sun Father and the will together. Here is the way it goes:

> The ones who were living in the fourth room
> were needed
>
> but
> the Sun was thinking
>
> he was thinking
> that he did not know what would happen now.

What does happen is the rain, the waterfall, and the sprouting of the twins from the foam. Then we are told, "Their father brought them to life," which points to the operation of will again; but the very next line simply says, "They came out of the suds," and we were previously told that they "sprouted." Whatever is at work here, or *not quite* at work, there is a meeting of the sunlight and the foam of the waterfall, and out come the twins. When the Sun Father tells the twins about the people of the fourth room, ourselves, he says:

> You will bring them out, and *perhaps then*
> as I have in mind
> they will offer me prayer-meal.

"Perhaps," he says, perhaps. The twins say this:

> We will *try*.
> This place where they may or may not live is *far*
> There in the room full of *soot*.

When they enter the fourth room and find the village there, they meet up with a person who happens to be out hunting. This is their first meeting with the *moss people,* the people who are living in total darkness but who are about to receive the Word of the Sun Father, the word that will project a world for them. This hunter they meet is a modest person; he speaks with a weak voice. But before they have explained their project, he remarks,

> Well, perhaps I
> might know why it is you came.

He takes them to the village, where they meet the Talking Priest, the Spokesman, and give him their "word of indeterminate importance" concerning emergence into the daylight. He responds:

> Indeed.
>
> But even if that is what you have in mind
> How will it be done?

And he even asks them directly: *"Do you have the means for getting out there* successfully?" To which they respond,

> *Well*
> well, no.

The Spokesman then suggests they call in the Priest of the North. But the Priest of the North doesn't know how to get out of the Soot Room and suggests the West Priest. The West Priest doesn't know and suggests the South Priest, and the South Priest suggests the East Priest, and the East Priest says, "I, least of *all.*" He suggests the twins, who brought the word in the first place: "Perhaps they know how to do this after all," he says, and they say,

> Well
> Well *I don't know.*
> But I will *try* something.

The twins take all the people along toward the east for a distance, and then go ahead of them a little. When they find themselves alone, one of them says to the other, "What are we going to do?" And the other makes a further suggestion, prefaced with a "perhaps." With just such questions and perhapses, they manage to find a way up through the third, second, and first rooms. In each room they plant a tree, and the branches of that tree form a spiral staircase into the next and lighter room. But the seeds of all plants were already all there in the dark, in the possession of the priests of the moss people.

When they are all in the first room beneath, where everything is the color of dawn, the twins make an announcement to the people:

> *Now you must step from branch to branch again*
> *until we come out, out into our Sun Father's daylight. Even*
> * though it will be hard*
> *you must do your best*
> to look at your father
> for you will hardly be able to *see*
> There in the room full of soot, when we entered upon your
> * roads, we could hardly *see.*
> That is the way it will be with you, *certainly.*[15]

So, just as the Ahayuuta could not see in the Soot Room, so the moss people will not be able to see in the daylight. This is the kind of thing that structural analysis is made of. But wait a minute; this is not a trade-off of opposites: "You will *hardly* be able to see," they say to the people; and they say of themselves in the Soot Room, "We could *hardly* see." The hunter they met there said, "Well, perhaps I might know why it is you came"; and the twins, the sons of the Sun Father and the bearers of his Word, said they would *try* something. And when the people finally come out of the last room, they come out not at midday as if expressing a direct opposition between darkness and light, but they come out at the same moment the sun *rises*. It is hard, but they *look at* their Sun Father. At daybreak.

Now the twins take the people eastward for some distance, the first step of a migration that will lead to the place where the town of Zuni now stands. The twins make an announcement:

> *"Now*
> we will stay here four days," they said. *They were going*
> *to stay four years.*
> *For four years they lived* where they had stopped.

So the twins say four *days*, but our narrator tells us they mean (or the text means) four *years*. Kyaklo does not tell us this, it is *not* in the *book*, but this particular detail is a part of *all interpretations*. It is like the comment of a scholiast in an ancient written text, but it has not become embedded in the text itself. At the same time, it is not set apart in a treatise on theology. It is not the subject of an argument over whether the Book really means seven days. What the Ahayuuta *say* is four *days*, and what they mean is four *years*. But there is something more here than just an explanation, a sort of translation, of the mysterious language of the Ahayuuta. We can't just say, "All right, they really mean four years," and be done with it. It still remains that they *said* four *days*. And if we look again, we see that our interpreter didn't say they *meant* four years. The Ahayuuta say, "We will stay here four days"; and the interpreter says, "They were going to stay four years." But this is not a deviation from *plan*, either. After the four years are up, the Ahayuuta say, "We've been here *four days*." But I don't want to say, therefore, that they *meant* four years, in some kind of code language. When we decode that we've got nothing left. We might as well erase "days" and replace it with "years." But our interpreter puts four days *alongside* four years;

and in fact he does it two different times, once at the opening of this episode and once at the close, just in case we might miss it.

Now, suppose we've heard an interpretation or two of "that which was the beginning," and we finally have an opportunity to go and listen to Kyaklo. When we hear him saying "four days," then we'll know . . . what will we know? Whatever we *think*, he *says* four days. But we can't stop knowing about the four years. Something is happening with time here, within time, something with its marking and its duration; and it is happening *between* the text and the interpretation. It seems like *ages*. It seems like only *yesterday*.

Who are these Ahayuuta, these twins, who talk like this? Their name is a clue because they both go by the same name, Ahayuuta, whereas no two living people should ever have the same name. Once in a great while the Ahayuuta reveal, as they do elsewhere in the present narrative, that they also possess separate names of their own; but they are as close as they could possibly be to the rift between being the same person and a different person. The Kyaklo text and all the interpretations tell us that although they are twins, one of them is the elder and the other is the younger. Of course: twins are born one at a time. But they are as close to the rift of elder and younger as they could possibly be. They are called Ahayuuta *an papa*, "the Ahayuuta's elder brother," and Ahayuuta *an suwe*, "the Ahayuuta's younger brother." They are named by reference to each other. If I refer to the elder brother, I am in effect naming his younger brother "Ahayuuta" and then saying that Ahayuuta has an elder brother. If I refer to the younger brother, I am in effect naming his elder brother "Ahayuuta" and then saying that Ahayuuta has a younger brother. What is called Ahayuuta is between them.

Neither text nor previous interpretations tell us what stage of life these Ahayuuta are in, beyond the fact that they are not fully grown; but now that we can listen to the voice of a narrator as he speaks their lines, rather than merely reading a conventional alphabetic transcription, we hear that the younger one has a high voice that tends to crack.[16] In other words, the two of them are differentiated by the rift of adolescence, even though they were almost born simultaneously.

The twins make everything possible; they are, in Heidegger's terms, "the rift of difference" itself. That rift, he says, "makes the limpid brightness shine,"[17] and this is the time to say that the

Ahayuuta carry weapons, and that those weapons are lightning. This is their *brilliance*. The people say they are *ayyuchi'an aaho''i*, "extraordinary, amazing beings." *Pikwayina* is the Zuni term for miracle; it means something like "pass through to the other side." If the rain comes through our roof, somehow, and a drop forms on the ceiling and falls, then *k'a pikwayi*, the rain has passed through to the other side. But the Ahayuuta say, "Extraordinary beings we are *not*." They're a little small for their age, they are dirty, they have lice in their hair. They sprouted from the alkaline foam of a muddy flash flood after a heavy rain. But "their Sun Father brought them to life." Is this their point of *origin*? Is the *will* of the Sun Father the first cause of all differences? Did everything begin with his word? But the world was already there, four rooms of people, already there, these people who might already know something. The Sun Father wants the people to come out of the fourth room, he has a desire in the matter; but he *does not know*, altogether and in advance, what will happen in the meeting of his will with what already is. And from there the Ahayuuta are "given life." Or: they *sprout*. What does it mean to say this is their origin, their starting point? The rain was not made, the earth was not made: they always already were. When we go beyond the Kyaklo text and its interpretations to the *tales* about the Ahayuuta, we again find something that's not in the *book*: in all of those tales, the Ahayuuta live with their grandmother.[18] Not with their mother—that would be the waterfall, we may guess—but with their mother's mother. They always already have a grandmother. And what is *her* name? She is simply called Ahayuuta *an hotta*, the Ahayuuta's grandmother. Of course. Grandmother of difference. She is the patroness of midwives. And what is her shining? The Sun Father gives daylight and the Ahayuuta travel on lightning. Whenever the Zunis touch a glowing coal to a cigarette, they say they are giving their grandmother a seat in the doorway.

So is *that* the starting of everything? Can we stop here, looking at the face of the Ahayuuta's grandmother? And what is that face? One side of her face is covered with ashes, and the other side is covered with soot. Ashes and fire are already there together. In the live coal, the ashes and soot are not waiting to be projected by the fire. Elder and younger are already there. The Sun and the people are already there. Desire and possibility are already there. The word and the world are already there. The text and the interpretation are already there.

Notes

1. For an explanation of the orthography used here, see Dennis Tedlock, *Finding the Center: Narrative Poetry of the Zuni Indians* (New York: Dial, 1972; rpt. Lincoln: University of Nebraska Press, 1978), pp. xxxiv-xxxv.

2. For a fuller discussion of the nonalphabetic features of the speaking (rather than chanting) voice, see Dennis Tedlock, "On the Translation of Style in Oral Narrative," *Journal of American Folklore* 84 (1971): 114-33; "Oral History as Poetry," *Boundary 2* 3 (1975): 707-26.

3. "Raising it right up" is treated in full in Dennis Tedlock, "From Prayer to Reprimand," in *Language in Religious Practice,* ed. William J. Samarin (Rowley, Mass.: Newbury House, 1976), pp. 72-83.

4. The lines of text and translation quoted here are my own revisions of the version of Matilda Coxe Stevenson, "The Zuni Indians," *Twenty-third Annual Report of the Bureau of American Ethnology* (Washington, D.C.: GPO, 1904), pp. 72-89, reprinted below, following these notes.

5. Stevenson, "Zuni Indians." This is not a complete version, but it gives a clear enough sense of the texture of the chant. For complete versions of other chants belonging to the same genre, see Ruth L. Bunzel, "Zuni Ritual Poetry," *Forty-seventh Annual Report of the Bureau of American Ethnology* (Washington, D.C.: GPO, 1932), pp. 710-76. My description of Kyaklo himself draws from Ruth L. Bunzel, "Zuni Katcinas," *Forty-seventh Annual Report of the Bureau of American Ethnology,* pp. 980-81, and from my own field notes dating from the period 1964-72.

6. For a summary of Zuni religious organization, see Dennis Tedlock, "Zuni Religion and World View," in *Handbook of North American Indians,* vol. 9, ed. Alfonso Ortiz (Washington, D.C.: Smithsonian Institution, 1979), pp. 499-508.

7. The version of the Priest of the East is given in Ruth L. Bunzel, "Zuni Origin Myths," *Forty-seventh Annual Report of the Bureau of American Ethnology,* pp. 549-602.

8. For an example of the weaving in of chance events, see Tedlock, *Finding the Center,* pp. 258, 271.

9. Dell Hymes, "Discovering Oral Performance and Measured Verse in American Indian Narrative," *New Literary History* 8 (Spring 1977): 441.

10. See Tedlock, *Finding the Center,* pp. 225-98, for a full translation.

11. This talk was given on the third floor of the School of Theology Building at Boston University. The Zunis themselves make the analogy between the stories of a building and those of the world. The priesthoods conduct their meditations four rooms beneath the top surface of the main building of the town, in total darkness.

12. See Ruth Benedict, *Zuni Mythology*, Columbia University Publications in Anthropology no. 21 (New York: Columbia University Press, 1935), 1:255-61, for a summary of previous versions.

13. All the passages quoted hereafter are from Tedlock, *Finding the Center*, pp. 225-98. Each change of line indicates a definite but brief pause, except for indented lines; pauses of two seconds or more are indicated by strophe breaks. In the passage quoted here, "a—ll" is pronounced with a prolongation of both the vowel and consonant.

14. Paul Ricoeur, *Interpretation Theory* (Fort Worth, Tex.: Texas Christian University Press, 1976), pp. 36-37.

15. The italics here indicate a louder voice.

16. See Tedlock, *Finding the Center*, pp. 168, 177, 179.

17. Martin Heidegger, *Poetry, Language, Thought,* tr. Albert Hofstadter (New York: Harper & Row, 1975), pp. 202-205.

18. See Dennis Tedlock, "The Girl and the Protector," *Alcheringa* 1, no. 1 (Spring 1975): 110-50, for a lengthy tale involving the Ahayuuta twins and their grandmother.

History Myth of the Coming of the A'shiwi as Narrated by Kyaklo

(Matilda Coxe Stevenson translation)

Narrator. Now we (the Zunis) come through the hole which is emptied of water for our passage and afterward fills with water, and we inhale the sacred breath of A'wonawil'ona. While we are in the fourth world, the blackness-of-soot world, our great fathers, Bow priests of the place, work for us. The elder brother does not care to perform the mysteries alone, but wishes his younger brother to join him in his wonderful work.

Elder brother. This light (pointing above) is what we are looking for. I have thought it all over. I want my younger brother of the place very much.

Narrator. The younger brother hastens.

Younger brother. Now, do you want me very much? What do you wish? What do you wish to say? Do you wish a great talk? All right; let me know what you wish to talk about.

Elder brother. I am thinking all the time of one thing; for many days I have concentrated my thoughts on the one thing; I am thinking seriously that I will remain here for a time to aid my people.

Narrator. The elder and younger brothers of the place talk to one another.
The two cut down the pine tree of the North (Pinus ponderosa); the two cut down the spruce (Pseudotsuga douglassii) of the West; the

two cut down the aspen (Populus tremuloides) of the South; the two cut down the silver spruce (Picca pungens) of the East.

Elder brother. Over there in the fourth (undermost) world, we sit down to talk together on serious subjects.

Over there in water-moss (third) world, we sat down to talk together on serious subjects.

Over there in mud (second) world, we sat down to talk together on serious subjects.

Over there in wing (sunbeam) (first) world, we sat down to talk together on serious subjects. Over there our fathers are nearby. We see all of our children; they are not happy there. It is dark inside; we can not see one another.

We step on one another's toes. We are looking for the light; all must look for it; this light (pointing above) we are looking for. I have thought it over; this is what you want very much; all wish our rain-priest father of the North.

Narrator. They talked to one another. The two wished the rain priest of the North very much.

He hastened, carrying his precious things clasped to his breast.

Elder brother. All wish our rain-priest father of the West.

Narrator. They talked together. The two wished the rain priest of the West very much. He hastened, carrying his precious things clasped to his breast.

Elder brother. All wish our rain-priest father of the South.

Narrator. They talk together. The two wish the rain priest of the South very much. He hastens, carrying his precious things clasped to his breast.

Elder brother. All wish our rain-priest of the East.

Narrator. They talk together. The two wish the rain priest of the East very much. He hastens, carrying his precious things clasped to his breast. They stoop over and come out through the place which was filled with water, the water disappearing for the time being to permit the A'shiwi to pass. The two meet.

Elder brother. All wish the Middle place; we must look for the Middle of the world; we are on the road. Our great fathers and our people stop here together.

Narrator. Our great fathers talked together. Here they arose and moved on. They stooped over and came out from the fourth world, carrying their precious things clasped to their breasts.

They stooped over and came out from moss world, carrying their precious things clasped to their breasts.

They stooped over and came out from the wing or sun rays world, carrying their precious things clasped to their breasts.

They stooped over and came out and saw their Sun Father and inhaled the sacred breath of the light of day.

Second-world place, third-world place, fourth-world place.

Following their road of exit, they stooped over and came out.

They walked this way.

They came to the gaming-stick spring.

They came to the gaming-ring spring.

They came to the Galaxy Fraternity baton spring.

They came to the spring with prayer plume standing.

They came to the cat-tail place.

They came to the moss spring.

They came to the muddy spring.

They came to the sun-ray spring.

They came to the spring by many aspens.

They came to shell place.

They came to dragon-fly place.

They came to flower place.

They came to the place of trees with drooping limbs.

They came to fish spring.

They came to young-squash spring.

They came to listening spring.

Our great father old dance man; our great mother old dance woman.

They possess much knowledge; they finished the rivers.

They possess much knowledge; they made Ko'thluwala'wa mountain.

Elder brother. All wish our great fathers, the Kia'ettowe, Chu'ettowe, Mu'ettowe, Hle'ettowe (rain and crop fetishes).

Narrator. They passed between the mountains. It is far to the Middle of the world.

Our great fathers! our great mothers!

Here we will sit perfectly still for days, which will be precious, and our hearts will speak with the gods of the inside water place; all wish to meet together.

Sun priest (deputy to Sun Father). Here we will sit perfectly still, not moving body or limb; where can we talk together?

Kia'kwemosi (Director-general of the House of Houses). Our priest of the Dogwood clan knows.

Sun priest. Much thought has been given to finding a place; one has been found; give no further thought to it.

Narrator. Our great fathers sit perfectly still. There we can talk with them. Now all my children are happy together.

Here we finish our prayer plumes.

There our fathers the Council of the Gods will receive them.

Pau'tiwa. Our great fathers, Kia'ettowe, Chu'ettowe, Mu'ettowe, Hle'ettowe, passed between the mountains to find the Middle of the world, where they sit perfectly still.

Who is a good man? Who possesses much wisdom?

A member of the Council of the Gods. Over there, in the room above, sitting in the hatchway. Everybody knows Kyaklo of the place; this man knows much.

Pau'tiwa. Now, I wish some one to tell him to come.

Narrator. He hastens, comes in, and sits down.

Kyaklo. I am here. What do you wish of me? You wished me to come. What do you wish to say? Do you wish to talk much together?

Pau'tiwa. There in I'tiwanna (Middle name place) our great fathers sit perfectly still.

You will tell the great ones to count the days one by one, and in eight days the gods will go over the road and meet all our fathers. We will go over the road and meet them; we will meet all our fathers.

Now, think of some. Perhaps all are gathered. Good! No, I have not my North father of the place, the god with the scapula of the yellow deer of the North; the god with the scapula of the blue deer of the West; the god with the scapula of the red deer of the South; the god with the scapula of the white deer of the East; the god with the scapula of the every-colored deer of the Zenith; the god with the scapula of the black deer of the Nadir.

I wish the god with wood ears on his mask very much.

I wish the god with the wool cap very much.

I wish the god possessing many deer very much.

I wish the god A'nahoho very much.

I wish the god Shu'laawisi very much.

I wish the gods who carry reed staffs ornamented with twigs of the spruce tree of the west very much.

I wish the shaker, (Kyaklo), the great dictator, who goes about, very much.

I wish all of the gods with blue-horned masks very much.

I wish the Plumed Serpent very much.

I wish the god Suti'ki very much.

I wish the suckling very much.

I wish the old dance men very much.

Great father of the Ko'yemshi. Now, do you want me very much?

Pau'tiwa (addressing great father Ko'yemshi). You will go over the road with Kyaklo and meet our fathers at the Middle place.

You will carry this for your rattle when you go to meet your fathers.

Narrator. Kyaklo comes out and sits down. He looks to the six regions and calls: "Kyaklo, Kyaklo, Kyaklo, Kyaklo grandfathers; where are you? Carry me on your backs."

The old dance men, hearing Kyaklo call, come from their mountains to the lake. Kyaklo mounts the back of the deputy to the great father of the old dance men, and looks to the six regions. Kyaklo looking to the east, sees four roads close together.

Kyaklo. We will take the middle road. We will come this way. Grandfathers, you will sing.

Narrator. Kyaklo now recounts the travels of the ancients to the Middle of the world.

Kyaklo. We come this way. We come to a large lake; here we get up and move on. We come to a valley with watercress in the middle; here we get up and move on.

We come to the stealing place; here we get up and move on.

We come to houses built in mesa walls; here we get up and move on.

We come to the last of a row of springs; here we get up and move on.

We come to the middle of a row of springs; here we get up and move on.

We come again to the middle of a row of springs; here we get up and move on.

We come to the house of Ko'loowisi; here we get up and move on.

We come to watercress place; here we get up and move on.

We come to a small spring; here we get up and move on.

We come to a spring in a hollow place in a mound, hidden by tall bending grasses; here we get up and move on.

We come to ashes spring; here we get up and move on.

We come to high-grass spring; here we get up and move on.

We come to rainbow spring; here we get up and move on.

We come to place of the Sha'lako; here we get up and move on.

We come to the place with many springs; here we get up and move on.

We come to moss place; here we get up and move on.

We come to stone-lodged-in-a-cleft place; here we get up and move on.

We come to stone-picture (pictograph) place; here we get up and move on.

We come to poison-oak place; here we get up and move on.

We come to a spring in a mesa wall; here we get up and move on.

We come to rush place; here we get up and move on.

We come to a place of bad-smelling water; here we get up and move on.

We come to the place of sack of meal hanging; here we get up and move on.

We come to the blue-jay spring; here we get up and move on.

We come to Corn mountain; here we get up and move on.

We come to the spring at the base of the mesa; here we get up and move on.

We come to the ant-entering place; here we get up and move on.

We come to vulva spring; here we get up and move on.

We come to a spring high in the mountain; here we get up and move on.

We come to Apache spring; here we get up and move on.

We come to coyote spring; here we get up and move on.

We come to salt place; here we get up and move on.

We come to a place with fumes like burning sulphur; here we get up and move on.

We come to ant place; here we get up and move on.

We come to the Middle place.

Kyaklo (addressing the A'shiwi). In a short time my fathers, whom I have there, will meet you on the road. You will meet together. They will come, and will give to all your children more of the great breath; the breath of A'wonawil'ona; the breath of the light of day.

BARRE TOELKEN and TACHEENI SCOTT

Poetic Retranslation and the "Pretty Languages" of Yellowman

Introduction

In recent years, Dell Hymes, Dennis Tedlock, and others have shown how line-by-line presentation of Native American oral literature allows for a fuller access to the original power and meaning of the stories by outsiders reading the works in translation.[1] This mode of presentation may properly be called "poetic," not because the right margin is uneven or because of any imagined special visual effect, but because each line is put forth in such a manner as to render its fullest available charge of texture: rhythm, nuance, phrasing and metaphor—factors which may depend partly on relation to other lines by parallelism, redundancy, grouping— without forced regard for the printer's convention of justified lines.

Perhaps it is our own literacy which has encouraged us over the years to *see* stories as things, as texts, rather than try to *hear* them as performances. In any case, we have generally been more concerned with efficient translations of texts, no matter how dull the result might be, than we have with renderings of performances, no matter how powerful even a partial success might be. Tedlock's work of translating directly from Zuni into lines showing volume and pitch has demonstrated what *is* possible when oral delivery is recomposed for recognition by the eye. Of course in this process much is lost, but how much is saved can be seen by comparing Hymes's work to Franz Boas's field collections.[2] It is not simply a matter of arranging "regular" oral prose into poetic-looking lines; rather, the translator is forced to deal with the full content in each line without taking refuge in the intellectual, explanatory possibilities of prose rationalization, forced to deal with dramatic directness without a comfortable recourse to indirect description.

Compare the following prose translation given by Boas of the Tsimshian story "The Grizzly Bear" with a poetic retranslation based on Boas's own transcription and interlinear phrase translation.[3] In this passage, the third of three brothers, described as "a great, awkward [perhaps 'improper'] man," has climbed up over a steep icy slope to where his two brothers—one at a time—have been pulled by a grizzly into her den and killed.

He went near, and had just placed himself in position when the great Grizzly Bear stretched out her arms, and the great man fell into the den headlong. Then he struck the Grizzly Bear and his hand got into her vulva. Then she said to her cubs, "My dear ones, make the fire burn brightly, for your father is cold." She felt much ashamed because the man had struck her vulva, therefore she felt kindly toward him, and did not kill him. She liked him. She said, "I will marry you." And the big man agreed. Then the great Grizzly Bear was very glad because the Indian had married her.

The following "retranslation" uses the wording and phrasing available in Boas's interlinear text of the same story. Each utterance is put down here as a separate line; and lines are grouped together by topic, action, and import, as defined partly by content, partly by phrasing and parallelism. Admittedly, this is rough guesswork; but even so, a more engaging—I think one may say exciting—dimension becomes available to us: the immediacy of dramatic presence. Added to that, the line-by-line scrutiny helps us recover the line, "Then always they lay down," which establishes an important setting of conjugal relationship—left out entirely in Boas's prose translation.

Then he just began to place himself well.
Then suddenly the great Grizzly Bear stretched out her paws.
Headfirst the great man went in.

Then this way he slapped it.
His hand got right into the great vulva
    of the great Grizzly Bear.

> Then said the great Grizzly Bear
> > to her cubs:
> "My dears! Make the fire burn very brightly—
> he begins to feel cold,
> > your father."
>
> Much ashamed was the heart of the great Grizzly Bear
> > because the great man felt in her vulva.
> Therefore it was very good for the man
> > that she not also killed him
> > because inside he had felt.
> Therefore she liked him.
>
> Then said the great Grizzly Bear:
> "I will marry you."
> Then agreed the great man.
>
> Very good in heart was the great woman Grizzly Bear
> > because he married her,
> > the great Indian.
>
> Then always they lay down.

At the close of the same story, after the bear and the man have gone to live in his village for a considerable time, the grizzly wife is scolded by a young man who resents her constant presence in the tribal fish trap. In Boas's prose:

Then the great Grizzly Bear took notice of it. She became angry, ran out, and rushed up to the man who was scolding her. She rushed into the house, took him, and killed him. She tore his flesh to pieces and broke his bones. Then she went. Now she remembered her own people and her two children. She was very angry, and she went home. Her husband followed her, but the great Grizzly Bear said, "Return home, or I shall kill you." But the man refused, because he loved his great wife. The Grizzly Bear spoke to him twice, wanting him to go back, but he refused. Then she rushed upon him and killed him, and her own husband was dead. Then the great Grizzly Bear left.

Following is the same passage, directly from Boas's interlinear presentation, taken line by line. Note how the indirect description and reportage in the above rendering disappears in the dramatic mode.

> Then she noticed it,
> > the great Grizzly Bear.

67

Then she came,
    being sick in heart.
Then quickly she ran out at him,
    greatly angry.

Then she went where the man was
    who scolded.
Then into that place she stood.

Then she took the man.
Then all over she killed him.
It was dead,
    the man.
All over was finished his flesh.
Then were broken all his bones.

At once she went.
She remembered her people
    where her two cubs were.
Then went the great Grizzly Bear.
Angry she was,
    and sick at heart.

Then her husband followed her.

Then the Grizzly Bear said this:
"Âdo! Turn back!
Maybe I will kill you!"

Then the man refused,
    because he loved the great wife Grizzly Bear.

Twice spoke the great Grizzly Bear;
    She sent her husband back

Then he refused.
Therefore she did it,
    the great Grizzly Bear
    rushed back.

Then she killed him.
Then was dead
    the man,
    her own husband.

Then the great Grizzly Bear left.

It was dead,
    the man.

This resetting of the piece does not take into consideration such presentational devices as would surely be discovered by close linguistic scrutiny. Hymes demonstrates, in "Discovering Oral Performance and Measured Verse in American Indian Narrative," that in Chinook stories initial elements like "Now," "Then," "Now then," are not random conversational connectors, but are the reference points to organizational elements which can be shown in print as "stanzas" and "verses." What is offered here for the Tsimshian story is a rough gathering of passages into scene and action groups, without reference to the richer evidence for even greater meaning and impact which lurks there on the page for someone with language facility to bring forth.

The stark drama of the poetic presentation is obviously more germane to the content and mood of the story's ending than the awkward reportage of the prose account. If it is true, as teachers of literature are wont to insist, that the *way* a thing is said is *part* of what is being said, then we cannot afford to slacken our attempts to determine what those *ways* are in every piece of native literature we seek to study, and what the relationships of those ways are to what is said and meant in each work.

At least it is with this aim in mind that I have encouraged—even forced—my students in recent years to go beyond mere reading of native literature and into the troublesome, frustrating, and often impossible task of recovering something of the original. "But what if we can't *speak* Tsimshian?" they ask: "How are we to presume we can reconstitute the original presentation properly?" My response is to suggest that—using the materials at hand—we can at least come *closer* to a real presentation than is now provided for us in the awkwardly serviceable and often primitive-sounding prose translations of linguists who were not anyhow as involved in the study of live literature as in the recovery of almost moribund languages.

Throughout this insistence, however, has run one disquieting thought for me: all of my own work with Navajo narratives has used prose as the medium of presentation. The one story which I have dealt with most fully in print—and which has brought positive responses from colleagues and specialists on Navajo language and culture—exists in prose even though my attempt in that article is to reveal the stylistic, presentational aspects of the story. With some trepidation I decided to follow my own advice and retranslate the piece to see what discoveries could be made about the story which *should* have been part of my original discussion. Some of my fears have been borne out: I have discovered patterns, words, and meanings that I did not see before; I have been forced to deal directly with matters I had easily buried in prose explanation; worst of all, I realized I had failed even to hear some words because I didn't think they were there. Discussion of the most important of these will be presented below.

The following article reproduces, unchanged except for some minor clarifications, the essay and prose translation of my earlier article, "The 'Pretty Languages' of Yellowman: Genre, Mode, and Texture in Navajo Coyote Narratives."[4] This will be followed by the newly retranslated text, provided in the poetic line-by-line form. My coauthor and cotranslator, Orville Tacheeni Scott, is a Navajo Ph.D. candidate in biology at the University of Oregon. We have gone through the 1966 tape recording of Yellowman's story several times together; without his help, this retranslation would have been entirely impossible for me. In addition, his elucidation of cultural and linguistic features of the story has provided the means of making legitimate and accurate analytic comments which otherwise would have remained unformed.

I.

The 1969 article is an expansion of a paper presented at the 1967 Annual Meeting of the American Folklore Society at Toronto. Travel grants to support recording and further study were provided by the Department of English and by the Office of Scientific and Scholarly Research of the University of Oregon. For supplying first aid to the author's failing Navajo language and for providing excellent comments on the nature of this investigation, I am deeply indebted to Annie and Helen Yellowman, daughters of the narrator, and to the Reverend Canon H. B. Liebler, longtime Episcopal missionary to the Navajos.

The story is this: Coyote, wishing to take revenge on prairie dogs for insulting him, persuades Skunk to help him deceive the small animals into thinking he is dead. Prairie dogs are killed and cooked; a race is proposed to see who will eat the cooked animals. Skunk runs out of sight, hides, and returns early, taking all but four small animals up to a ledge where he eats them, later throwing scraps down to Coyote.

Probably no other character is encountered throughout such a broad range of Navajo legend, chant, and folktale as Ma'i (Coyote).[5] Yet, even though he has been the subject of scholarly comment in nearly every serious ethnographic investigation of Navajo culture and literature, a close critical analysis of Ma'i in Navajo lore, based on good data, has yet to appear. The scope of such a study is of course far beyond the capabilities of a single essay, or probably of a single writer. Some literary observations on the narratives, however, are possible at this time: because these narratives appear in such a wide spectrum of Navajo tradition, it is obvious even to someone of my limited acquaintance with them that their stylistic attributes reach far beyond the so-called Coyote Tale and into the whole concept of Navajo literary expression.

For purposes of focus here I will illustrate my remarks primarily by reference to tales told by one Navajo raconteur. In spite of the severe limitations we must place on generalizing from the data provided by one informant, I would rather work from material I have collected myself (for reasons which will become more apparent below) and from comments made to me by a single good informant than to cope badly with the uncountable critical problems which arise in the use of transcribed texts, no matter how serious or how august their collector may have been. The Navajo propensity toward playing subtle tricks on outsiders on the one hand, or the occasional attempt, on the other, to apologize rhetorically for one's own very knowledge of the tales (for example, overuse of the term *jiní*, "they say"[6]), when added to the already dizzying profusion of transcription techniques, makes the close literary use of published texts critically hazardous for anything beyond synopses.

For another kind of focus, directly related to the fact that this is an essay, not an anthology of Navajo tales, I will use one particular tale as an examplar of the literary conditions I plan to discuss. The reader will have to trust my choice of this tale as, first, typical of the Coyote stories, and, second, as broadly representative of the stylistic and structural matters which are not always present in every tale but which become familiar to one who has heard many of the tales over a period of time. Admittedly, even such brief remarks as I can make here will be a considerable load for such small evidence; the aim of this piece, then, is to be provocative, not definitive. Even so, the observations I make here, as far as I can check them through other data available to me, are not exceptional in nature to those which could be made were I to offer twenty or fifty such tales as textual evidence.

First, a word about the narrator and my acquaintance with him, since these matters have an important bearing on the reliability of the data and on my position as the collector and evaluator of them. It has been my distinct good fortune to have lived among the Navajos on the Northern Reservation (chiefly in southern Utah) off and on for thirteen years, for three of these years under the most intimate conditions, and for nearly all of one of these years (1955–56) as an adopted member of a family who lived far from roads (in the then remote Aneth district, in Montezuma Canyon) and who spoke no English. This was the family of Tsinaabąąs Yazhi (Little Wagon) which consisted of an old man and his wife (in their 70's), their daughter (then about twenty-five years old), her husband, Yellowman (then about forty), and several of their small children. My adoption by the old man put me in the position of participating fully in the entire activities of the family.[7]

During a rather severe winter we spent most evenings sitting around the fire in Little Wagon's large hogan listening to the old man tell tales, legends, and miscellaneous yarns. It was under these circumstances that I first observed, albeit unwittingly, something of key importance about Navajo mythic narrative. A small family passing by on horseback had stopped for the night, according to the usual custom. Outside it had begun to snow lightly, and one of the travelers' children asked where snow came from. Little Wagon, in answer, began a long and involved story about an ancestor who had found a piece of beautiful burning material, had guarded it carefully for several months until some spirits (ye'i) came to claim it, and had asked then that the spirits allow him to retain a piece of it. This they would not allow, but they would see what they could do for him. In the meantime he was to perform a number of complicated and dedicated tasks to test his endurance. Finally, the spirits told him that in return for his fine behavior they would throw all the ashes from their own fireplace down into Montezuma Canyon each year when they cleaned house. Sometimes they fail to keep their word, and sometimes they throw down too much; but in all, they turn their attention toward us regularly, here in Montezuma Canyon. When this long story had been completed, there was a respectful silence for a moment; and then the young questioner put in: "It snows at Blanding, too. Why is that?" "I don't know," the old man replied immediately. "You'll have to make up your own story for that." I of course now assumed that the whole story had been made up for the occasion, and so it seemed; but I have encountered other students of the Navajos since then who have heard the same or a similar story. The literary point came to me later, as Little Wagon commented after the travelers' departure that it was too bad the boy did not understand stories. I found by questioning him that he did not in fact consider it an etiological story, and did not in any way believe that that was the way snow originated; rather, if the story was "about" anything, it was about moral values, about the deportment of a young protagonist whose actions showed a properly reciprocal relationship between himself and nature. In short, by seeing the story in terms of any categories I had been taught to recognize, I had missed the point; and so had our young visitor, a fact which Little Wagon at once attributed to the deadly influences of white schooling.

In these nightly sessions Little Wagon usually held the floor, with his son-in-law, Yellowman, telling only a few tales now and then. It was not until twelve years later, when Yellowman had moved his family to Blanding, Utah (after two desperate years of near starvation on the reservation) that I visited him during the winter when the tales can be told and found him now an apparently inexhaustible source of tales, legends, astronomy, and string figures, narrating almost nightly to his family with a finesse I have not encountered in any other informant. Yellowman has now had thirteen children, and all of those old enough have gone to school. Yet English is not spoken by the children at home; and although Yellowman now lives in a frame house on the edge of town, has made moccasins at the Utah State Fair, works for the Forest Service during the summers, and has numerous contacts with whites, he still prefers not to speak English—probably out of cultural aloofness. He still brings up his children in the Navajo way, still dances in the *Ye'i bichei* ceremony each year, carries his babies in a cradleboard, and acts the part of a cultural adviser to many nearby Navajos. His wife still grinds corn and berries on a flat stone, dresses and weaves in traditional fashion, cooks and serves the usual Navajo fare: coffee, mutton, *náneeskaadí* (a tortillalike dry bread). Because of these and many other elements of cultural conservatism, as well as for his striking talents at story-telling, I consider Yellowman an outstanding and, for our pur-poses, culturally reliable informant. In addition, he has shown a very cheerful willingness to respond to questions about Navajo stories and storytelling; thus I have been able to check on a number of matters which otherwise would have remained quite indistinct in my mind.[8]

I have mentioned these details at length because they have much to do with the kind of evidence I mean to bring forth in this article. Most anthropological data on the Navajos I have read to date are plagued, as suggested partially above, by two great areas of distortion: the first is the well-known tendency of our culture to see things chiefly in terms of its own existing categories, and thus to classify data in its own terms. This leaning may have as much to do with normal thought processes as it does with cultural myopia, and we may never be able to cure it; but we should be aware of its effects on what we suppose to be our objectivity.[9] The second possibility for distortion lies in the Navajo view of information and how it may be transmitted. Sometimes an *atti-tude* may be accurately communicated in a statement which is technically false, but which uses humor as a vehicle (such as when an elderly Navajo began to refer to me as his grandfather because of my beard); sometimes aloofness or an unwillingness to be im-pressed is communicated by statements designed to make the listener appear stupid or to imply he has missed the point of one's remark (such as when a man heard me say I was from the East—literally, from near where the sun comes up—and commented, as if to someone else, "It must be pretty hot there"); still other infor-mation which may fall into a rather large ritual category must be specifically requested four times (the Navajo "special" number), or it will not be given. David F. Aberle found, for example, that some of his information relating to peyotism was affected by his initial unawareness that some potential informants assumed his single question indicated he did not really want an answer. Very likely he assumed they were reluctant to answer, and like a gentleman changed the subject.[10] I cannot safely say that my own work is immune to such problems, or to still others I have not myself isolated or yet recognized; but my firsthand experience with Navajo humor, my presence (and occasional participation) at a good number of Navajo ceremonials, and my continued and ready access to my adoptive family have made me sensitive to such areas when it has come to making generalizations about the data.

With these preliminary remarks, then, let me present a typical "Coyote tale" for consideration here. The narrator's actions, styles, and devices will appear in parentheses, the audience's reactions in brackets. These references will make it necessary to place information such as linguistic comments in footnotes; since this is at best a burden on the reader, I will provide notes only for those points which bear on the story or on the subsequent discussion of it. The story is one I identify descriptively by characters and plot direction, for to my knowledge it has no formal title: Coyote, with the aid of Skunk, plays dead in order to kill and eat some prairie dogs.[11] This particular text was recorded at Blanding, Utah, on the evening of December 19, 1966, as Yellowman told the tale to several of his children; the translation which appears here was made with the valuable help of Annie Yellowman during the summer of 1968, for use in this article.

(style: slow, as with factual conversational prose; regular intonation and pronunciation; long pauses between sentences, as if tired) Ma'i was walking along once[12] in a once-forested area named after a stick floating on the water. He began walking in the desert in this area, where there were many prairie dogs, and as he passed by them they called him mean names, but he ignored them. He was angry, even so, and it was noon by then, so he made a wish:

(slower, all vowels more nasalized) "I wish some clouds would form." He was thinking about killing these prairie dogs, so he wished for clouds, and there were clouds. [audience: smiles and silent laughter]

Then he said: "I wish I could have some rain."[13] He said: "I wish the ground to be damp enough to cool off my hot feet." So the rain came as he wished, and cooled off his feet.[14]

"Now I want a little more, so the water will come up between my toes." [audience: quiet amusement, exchange of glances] Every time Ma'i wishes for something it comes about.

(pause, four seconds) "Now I want the water to come up to my knees." When it reached his knees, he wanted it to be even deeper so that only a small part of his back would show. Then he said: "I wish the water would rise some more so that only the tips of my ears will show." [audience: amusement, heavy breathing (to avoid open laughter)] Now he began to float. Then he said: "I wish I could float until I come to a stop along with some flood debris near the middle of the prairie dogs' area." [audience: quiet laughter] So that happened.

The pile of debris was made up of sticks, pine cones, and other fragments of vegetation, and mud. When he came floating to that place it had stopped raining. Ma'i lay there for a long while, pretending he was dead.

Skunk[15] was on his way by that place to get some water. [audience: silent laughter, knowing looks] Ma'i was pretending he was drowned [audience: quiet amusement] and Skunk didn't know he was there. [audience: open laughter; two girls now giggling almost constantly throughout the rest of this scene] Skunk had a dipper, and put it into the water.

"Shiłna'ash."[16] (Yellowman speaking very nasally, through side of mouth, lips unmoving and eyes closed, in imitation of Ma'i) [audience: open laughter, lasting three or four seconds].

Skunk turned around in fright, but he didn't see anyone. So he put his dipper in the water again, and Ma'i said:

"Shiłna'ash." (nasal, eyes closed, mouth unmoving, as before) [audience: quiet laughter] He said it four times,[17] and on the fourth time Skunk came to that place where Ma'i was lying. (using normal intonation)

(still nasal, lips unmoving, eyes closed, for Ma'i's speech) "Go back to the village and tell the prairie dogs that you were on your way to get water and you came across the body of a dead coyote that got drowned, shiłna'ash. Tell them 'It looks to me like he's been there for some time because it looks rotten and wormy.' Before you go there, get some t'loh ts'osi[18] and stick some under my arms, in my nose, in the corners of my mouth [audience: mild amusement], in my ears [audience: quiet laughter], in the joints of my legs; tell them how rotten I look. Tell them, 'He must have come down the wash and got drowned.' [audience: quiet laughter] And one last thing before you go there: go make some clubs, four of them, and put them under me. Tell them: 'Since the coyote is dead, why don't we go over there where he is and celebrate?'[19] When they get here, have them dance around in a circle. Keep one of the clubs, and when the prairie dogs beat me with their clubs, you do it, too. When they start dancing and beating, don't forget to tell them to take it easy on me; beat me slowly and not too hard," he said. [audience: laughter]

(normal tone) So Skunk went back to the prairie dogs' village and told the whole story as he was directed by Ma'i. He said: "I was just now on my way to get water and I came across the body of a dead coyote that got drowned. It looks to me like he's been there a long time because it looks rotten and full of worms. He must have come down the wash and got drowned. Why don't we go over there and have a ceremonial to celebrate his death?"

(normal conversational tone, perhaps a bit more slowly pronounced than usual) At the village there were also jackrabbits, cottontails, ground squirrels, and other small animals that Ma'i usually likes to eat. They couldn't believe it. They said: (nasal, high pitch) "Is it really true?" "Is it true?" "Is it true?" "I don't know; why doesn't someone besides Skunk go over there and see?"[20] (back to regular discourse, somewhat nasalized) So the jackrabbit went over to where Ma'i was and came back and told them it was all true. Then the cottontail went over there and came back and said it was all true. Then one of the prairie dogs went over there and came back and said: "It's true." On the fourth time they all went over there and gathered around Ma'i to celebrate. They began to dance around him; we don't know exactly what they were singing, but the noise sounded like they were all saying "Ma'i is dead" as they danced around and beat him slowly and gently. As they danced, more of them came along, and Skunk began to get ready to say what Ma'i had told him to say when he said: "Don't forget to do all these things at this time, shiłna'ash."

(Nasal whine) Skunk said then: "Look! Way, way up there is a *t'ajiłgai*[21] far above us." He said it four times, so the prairie dogs all looked up, and Skunk let out his scent[22] into the air and it came down right into their eyes. [audience: laughter] So the prairie dogs were fooled and they were busy rubbing their eyes.

Then Ma'i jumped up and said: "How dare you say I'm dead?" [audience: laughter][23] He grabbed the clubs under him and began to club the prairie dogs. [audience: laughter and giggling] He clubbed all the prairie dogs to death. [audience: extended laughter, including Yellowman (for the first time)]

(pause, after laughter, about four seconds)

"Let's start roasting the prairie dogs, shiłna'ash. You dig out a place in the sand."[24] So Skunk began to dig a place, and build a fire, and he put the prairie dogs in to cook.

"Let's have a race, shiłna'ash. Whoever gets back first can have all the fat prairie dogs." [audience: laughter]

(nasal whine) "No, I don't want to. My legs aren't long enough."

But Ma'i insisted. Skunk complained that he couldn't run as fast as Ma'i, so Ma'i gave him a head start. So Skunk ran off. Skunk ran beyond a hill and hid under a rock.[25] Soon after that, Ma'i passed by, running as fast as he could. He had tied a burning stick to his tail so as to make lots of smoke.[26] [audience: laughter, including Yellowman]

Skunk watched until Ma'i had gone completely out of sight, and then went back to where the prairie dogs were buried. (from this point on until midway in the next scene, the narration gets faster, with pacing related entirely to audience reaction, much in the manner of a "stand-up" comedian in a night club) He dug up all but the four skinniest prairie dogs and took them up onto a nearby ledge. [laughter] And while he was eating he watched for Ma'i, who soon came running as fast as he could. [laughter, including Yellowman] He wanted to make a good finish to show how fast he was, so he came running very rapidly and jumped right over the fire. [laughter, including Yellowman]

"Whew!!" he said. [peak laughter, much extended, including Yellowman] "Shiłna'ash, the poor old man with the stinking urine is still coming along." [extended laughter] Even though he was anxious to begin eating, he didn't want to look greedy, so he paced back and forth in the shade making lots of footprints which would show he had waited for a long time. [laughter, including Yellowman]

Then Ma'i went to the fire and began digging with a stick to find the prairie dogs. He found a tail from one of the small prairie dogs and pulled on it. "Oh oh, the tail must have come loose from being overdone." [laughter] He took out the skinny carcass and threw it over his shoulder toward the east, and said: "There will be fatter ones than this."[27] [laughter]

Now, digging around with the stick,[28] he came onto the second skinny prairie dog and threw it toward the south, and said: "There will be fatter ones here."

(far more slowly, almost drowsily) He came to the third one and threw it toward the west, and the fourth one he threw toward the north. Then he dug around and around with the stick and couldn't find anything. He walked around and around and finally decided to go find those skinny ones he threw away. So he ate them after all. [quiet laughter]

Then he started looking for footprints.[29] [quiet laughter] After a long time he found some tracks leading away from the roasting area to the rock ledge. He walked back and forth along this line several times without seeing Skunk, until Skunk dropped a small bone down from the ledge. [quiet laughter]

Ma'i looked up. (nasal whine) "Shiłna'ash, could I have some of that meat given back to me?" [quiet laughter] He was begging, with his eyes looking upward. [laughter, including Yellowman]

(pause, seven seconds)

(admonishing tone, very slowly delivered) "Certainly not,"[30] said Skunk to the begging coyote. He finally dropped some bones down and Ma'i gnawed on them. [moderate laughter]

(pause, about five seconds)

That's what they say.[31]

Lawrence Hennigh has demonstrated recently the decisive importance of informant commentary in our critical approaches to the understanding of folktales which might seem at first easily classifiable in our terms; his study shows vividly that any consideration of folktale meaning made without reference to the informant's own critical and cultural observations is not only weak, but actually invites error.[32] Even though oral informants often disagree on the nature of the same materials, and even though it is probably impossible for a literate, scholarly audience ever to approach an oral tale from an oral culture with anything like a traditional mental "set," no matter how much informant material is available, we still may say that the informant's conception of his own art can open possibilities to us which we might otherwise never suspect, and can save us from the blunder of inserting our own culture's aesthetic prejudices where his belong. With these possibilities and limitations in mind, it is instructive to look into some areas of literary discussion which have come up in my conversations with Yellowman.

For one thing, I had noticed that a good many words and phrases used in the Ma'i stories were not familiar to me from regular conversational Navajo. I had found when I played tapes of these stories to Father H. B. Liebler, a man with some twenty years' fluency in Navajo, that he too missed a good part of the meaning.[33] I asked Yellowman, therefore, if he used a special vocabulary when he told the tales. His answer, not surprisingly, was yes; his explanation was essentially that these were "older" words and phrases, and that he used them because they were the vocabulary he had always heard used in the tales.[34] But then he added with a smile a comment which I have taken to mean: "They are beautifully old-fashioned." Certainly, the Navajo reverence for beauty and for ancient things is well known; but a slightly new dimension emerged when I talked with Yellowman's children about this matter. They reported that the vocabulary was so familiar to them that they understood it readily (they had heard it so often), that it did seem to add the valued sense of antiquity to the stories, but that in addition it lent to the narratives a kind of pleasant humor, a comfortable quaintness that seemed to provide (this is my interpretation of their remarks) a ready context for the humorous scenes within the story. The element of humor will come into deeper consideration below.

When I asked if he told the tale exactly the same way each time, he at first answered yes; but when evidence from compared tapes was brought into the discussion, it became clear that he had understood me to be asking him if he changed the nature of the prototype tale of his own volition; the wording was different each time because he recomposes with each performance, simply working from his knowledge of what ought to happen in the story and from his facility with traditional words and phrases connected, in his view, with the business of narrating Ma'i stories. He did not mention it, but it is quite obvious from tapes made of his stories when no children were present that the audience plays a central role in the narrative style; without an audience, his tales are almost entirely lacking in the special intonations, changes in speed, pacing, and dramatic pauses which are so prominent in the specimen text given above. Speaking in solitude to a tape recorder, Yellowman gives only a rather full synopsis of characters and incidents; the narrative drama, far from being memorized verbatim, emerges in response to the bona fide storytelling context.

Does Yellowman consider these to be chiefly children's stories? Not at all, although he spends more time telling them to his own children than to anyone else. Adults in the audience do not remove themselves; they are as emotionally involved as the children. And, as Yellowman points out, stories of Coyote and his role in the creation, emergence, and placement of stars, and in the continuing fortunes of men and animals, are told during the most serious of adult circumstances (that is, in ceremonies, myth recitations, chant explanations, and so forth) because he is an extremely important personage in the Navajo belief system.

Why, then, if Coyote is such an important mythic character (whose name must not even be mentioned in the summer months), does Yellowman tell such funny stories about him? Yellowman's answer: "They are not funny stories." Why does everyone laugh, then? "They are laughing at the way Ma'i does things, and at the way the story is told. Many things about the story are funny, but the story is not funny." Why tell the stories? "If my children hear the stories, they will grow up to be good people; if they don't hear them, they will turn out to be bad." Why tell them to adults? "Through the stories everything is made possible."[35]

Why does Coyote do all those things, foolish on one occasion, good on another, terrible on another? "If he did not do all those things, then those things would not be possible in the world." Yellowman thus sees Coyote less as a Trickster per se and more as an enabler whose actions, good or bad, bring certain ideas and actions into the field of possibility, a model who symbolizes abstractions in terms of real entities. Moreover, Freud notwithstanding, the narrator is in large part conscious of this function.[36] When in one story Coyote loses his eyes in a gambling match or gets them caught on a tree branch during a game, he replaces them with amber pitch balls, and the story ends by explaining, "That's how Ma'i got his yellow eyes." But I exasperated Yellowman on one occasion by pursuing the question of how coyotes could actually see if their eyes were made of amber balls. It turned out just as it had with Little Wagon's snow story: the essence of the tale was not on the surface at all. Yellowman explained patiently that the tale allows us to envision the possibility of such things as eye disease, injury, or blindness; it has nothing to do with coyotes in general; and Ma'i himself may or may not have amber eyes, but since he can do anything he wants to, the question is irrelevant—he has eyes and he sees, period. I have found since that time that most Navajos of my acquaintance know the story, with minor variations, and none of them takes it to be etiological.

On the basis of such comments as these (and there are many more like them in my notes), I can suggest several important things: that Coyote tales are not simply entertainment; that they are phrased consciously in such a way as to construct an interesting surface plot which can act as entryway to a more subtle and far more important area of consideration; that the telling of, and listening to, Coyote stories is a serious business with serious consequences, no matter how much the humor might lead an outsider to feel otherwise; that, in short, the structures and styles we find meaningful in lettered literature are likely to be misleading, or at least irrelevant. I am suggesting that the significant part of the Coyote stories resides in their texture, not their structure, and that excessive attention to structure and stated content may actually stand in the way of our seeing those subtle moral implications and conceptual patterns which seem to be the Navajos' main reasons for telling the story. For one thing, such approaches in the past have led to statements even by strong scholars like Clyde Kluckhohn, who said of Navajo narratives: "Folk tales are secular in that, although things happen in them which could never occur in ordinary life and are hence part of the supernatural order of events, they are told primarily for amusement and entertainment. . . .

Folk tales have none of the high seriousness of the myths."[37] Or the statement by W. W. Hill: "Navajo folklore can be divided into two principal parts: accounts which deal with religious subjects, and stories with morals but which are told primarily for amusement."[38] If both of these do not misunderstand what the Navajos consider a religious subject, they at least do not detect those textural elements which might have connected amusement with religion.

Alan Dundes has suggested that texture in a traditional text is the language employed: the particular phonemes, morphemes, rhymes, stresses, tones, pitches, and so on.[39] I would expand this somewhat and describe texture as *any* coloration given a traditional item or statement as it is being made. In narrative it would certainly include linguistic features, as well as any verbal manipulations which evoke, suggest, and describe, or those which in any way qualify, modify, expand, or focus the rational structure by reference to or suggestion of emotions, mores, traditional customs and associations, aesthetic sensitivities and preferences, and so on.[40]

Dundes is correct in pointing out that "the more important the textural features are in a given genre of folklore, the more difficult it is to translate an example of that genre into another language";[41] And, I would add, the more difficult it is for an outsider even to understand what, in fact, the given item or text means in its own language, and the more difficult it is to delineate genre (since genre, in our culture at least, is usually distinguished on the basis of structure). Admittedly, the concept of genre in our own culture has been cloudy. When we have been able to see clear differences in the way things look on paper (even or uneven right-hand margin) or in fields of focus (novel *vs.* short story), we have been able to make some clear distinctions. But there remains a considerable gulf between those who, like René Wellek and Austin Warren, classify on the basis of form and structure,[42] and those like Northrop Frye who prefer "the radical of presentation."[43] This has complicated our approach to the oral literatures of people for whom the material is not limited to particular forms (especially visible ones) and for whom the radical of presentation is always oral and dramatic.

I found in questioning Yellowman that his own concept of the Coyote materials was based almost exclusively on style, rather than on content or structure. Among other questions, I asked him how he would recognize the difference between a Coyote story and someone talking about Coyote if he were to hear only part of the total text; I asked if it would be possible, by listening to a tape recording, to detect the difference between a Coyote story told within a myth, during a chant, or to someone's family. To the first question, he replied that conversations about Coyote would not use the "ancient" words one would associate with the tales: at least subject matter is not distinctive. To the second, he replied that Coyote stories would be told about the same way under all circumstances, but that one might detect differing kinds of audience reaction. On these and other topics it became increasingly clear to me that Yellowman sees the Coyote stories not as narratives (in our sense of the term) but as dramatic presentations performed within certain cultural contexts for moral and philosophical reasons.[44] He does not therefore place the materials in separate categories except with respect to the way they are performed; that is, his central consideration is not one of structure/genre but of texture/mode, not because he is unaware of genre (for he distinguishes clearly among song, ceremonial chant, story, and oratory), but because in the case of the Coyote materials generic distinctions are far less relevant than are those textural keys which allow the listeners to gain access to the important levels of meaning.

Following Yellowman's lead here, let us take a closer look at some of the more easily discernible textural elements in the tale presented above. Probably most noticeable are the various recitative devices suggested by my descriptive comments in parentheses. These include a dramatic intonation put on by the narrator as he takes the parts of central characters, especially a slow nasalization of Ma'i's lines; a kind of nasalized delivery of all vowel sounds throughout the story (this may be a part of the "archaism" effect); a variation in phrasing, in which the opening and closing of the story are delivered quite slowly while the climax is in a passage of rapid delivery; the use of appropriate gestures, facial expressions, and body positions in taking the parts of various central characters; and, very importantly, a kind of contractual interaction which is developed by the narrator with his audience, which tends to direct these other aspects of recitation and which seems based in their mutual recognition of the story type, its central characters and their importance in the Navajo world view, and their expectation that this particular performance will cause important ideas to come alive in exciting ways.

Another aspect of texture is, of course, language; and in this department, without recourse to the special print necessary to make clear the fine shades of oral Navajo, we are limited to a few broad comments. Of basic importance to our understanding of the effect of the Coyote materials on a native audience is the observation that Navajo has no indirect discourse, and it has nothing quite like our infinitive. Thus, one does not say, "He said that he would come"; rather, one says, "'I will come,' he said." Similarly, if one is asking another if he needs help, one does not say, "Do you want me to help you?" Instead, one says: "'Help me,' is that what you mean to say?" In other words, one must think of how the *other* person would ask it, then say it that way, and add *nínízinya?*—which is often translated, "you want it?" but really means something more like: "Is that what you have in mind?" This is a linguistic feature, not an artistic device; nonetheless, in dialogue where there are questions being asked, or where information is imparted, especially in scenes where Coyote is trying to trick or take advantage of someone else, this formation, in company with the audience's appreciation and perception of the dramatic context, produces humorous irony. I have already mentioned the intentional use of language patterns for their pleasantly archaic effects on the story, and they need not be treated again here. There is, between these two areas, another interesting facet of artistic manipulation of a native linguistic feature: in the text above, there are three scenes in which there is an unusual overabundance of the nasal *ǫǫ* in the words chosen by the narrator.[45] This is a sound which occurs naturally in a number of Navajo words, and one which I have heard used widely in informal conversation by itself as an equivalent to the word for "yes": *Aoo'.* Often it is used, in my experience, while someone else is talking, by way of assent, or in order to show one is listening and following—much in the same way one uses *mhm* in informal English. Its implication, when used alone, is "That's correct," or "I agree," or "Yes, I understand." In the Coyote tales of Yellowman, there is a heavy use of words containing this sound in passages where Coyote is illustrating (by observance or nonobservance) some Navajo taboo, in passages where truth is being discussed, and in passages which seem to contain some key action in the development of the story line. There may be other appearances of this device, but I have not been able to catalog them clearly, mainly because the sound itself is fairly well distributed throughout all the texts I have collected; but suddenly one hears perhaps a whole sentence, or as many as three or four sentences, which feature this vowel sound almost to the total exclusion of others. In the tale above, the first such scene is the one in which the small animals are trying to determine the truth of Skunk's report of Ma'i's death; the second instance is the scene in which Skunk hides under a rock and we know he will be the first to claim the roasted prairie dogs (this would be the climax of the surface story, and will be discussed below); the third use of nasal *gq* comes in strongly as Ma'i begins to exhume the skinny prairie dogs and moves into position for his comeuppance. The impact of such passages is at least threefold: first, on the story (structural) level, we have a morpheme used as part of a word which communicates a particular meaning, with its normal range of denotation and connotation; secondly, we have on the "moral" (textural) level a morpheme used to suggest certainty, reliability, "truth" within the local context; thirdly, we have a complicated set of reactions based on the combination of the other two levels, for while we get a subliminal chant that implies, "Yes, there it is, now we know, this is what they say," we are perceiving simultaneously the irony of the situation—which in nearly every case is based on our recognition that things are not as the story characters see them: Coyote is not dead, a race is not really in progress (and betrayal is at hand), and the gluttonous Coyote gets finally four skinny and sandy prairie dogs. There is, in short, a simultaneous assignment of two different phonemes by use of the same morpheme; since it is done consciously and in particular story contexts, since it is done with the same intent each time (insofar as one can determine such things), and since the effects are quite appropriate to the dramatic context, it is difficult to believe that it happens by accident. The morpheme, nasal *gq*, would seem to constitute a usable, understandable textural formula which establishes a bridge between story and meaning by helping to create irony.

Another great body of textural reference lies in the area of traditional and cultural association, that is, in those words, colors, sequences, and actions which inevitably bring about reactions based on cultural values, mores, customs, and so on. The sequence of fours, as noted above, is—for a Navajo audience—loaded with traditional associations. Not only does a Navajo audience see in the sequence an automatic progression ending on something important at the fourth step, but the ritualism of four-ness in so many other areas of Navajo life now carries over to suggest an almost ceremonial significance for the actions of the characters in the tales. More subtle, for the outsider at any rate, is the high incidence of broken customs, or traditions ignored and transgressed. Admission of hunger or tiredness is considered an extreme weakness, and is subject to laughter;[46] begging help from someone of lesser talents (as Coyote does in the above tale) is idiotic, and is subject to ridicule; begging for food is contemptible, and brings laughter; any kind of extreme like overinquisitiveness, obtrusiveness, intrusiveness, gluttony, and so on, is considered the kind of weakness which must be cured by ceremony, and is often in the meantime subject to laughter—especially when it has been carried out by someone who should know better; betrayal in return, if portrayed as a comeuppance in kind, is considered funny; in addition to these considerations, any trick is thought to be funny in itself, no matter by whom or on whom it is played.

If we consider even these few textural possibilities and their presumable impacts on a traditional Navajo audience, and if we play them off against what we see happening on the structural (plot) level, we will find that the structure has acted simply as the vehicle. The structural climax, that point at which we can see the outcome of the story line—that is, when Skunk hides and then doubles back to get the prairie dogs—brings an appreciative look to the faces of the audience, but their heavy laughter begins when Ma'i goes racing by with his self-confident torch blazing. And the heaviest laughter of all comes when Ma'i throws himself down, exhausted, and reveals his weariness by saying, "Whew!!" It is not enough to point out that because the audience has heard the story so many times before it already knows the outcome; after all, the "Whew!!" has been heard many times before as well. What it indicates, I think, is that the audience's attention throughout is on Ma'i, his actions, and his reasons for those actions, that is to say, on culturally moral subjects which have little to do with "how the story comes out." To put it another way, the attention is chiefly on texture; and the textural climax comes when Ma'i, in a strong symbolic tableau of all weaknesses and excesses brought out in the narrative, provides a "releaser" for all the laughter which has been built up through the story. What might seem to us a frivolous action not directly related to plot development turns out to be, for the native audience, symbolic of the central concern of the story.

What remains, then, is to posit some relationship between humor, as we have seen it operate above, and "meaning" in the Coyote materials. W. W. Hill suggested that Navajo humor was used in religious contexts in a secondary way, to prevent a "lag in interest," but that in "lay stories" humor was centrally present for amusement's sake. Thus, for Hill, humor in Navajo ceremony was a digression, even though he did note that humorous episodes are often integral parts of ritual acts and in spite of the fact that one informant pointed out to him that "it was not done just because of the fun; it was a part of the ceremony."[47] Hill did, however, recognize something of extreme importance in the social function of Navajo humor: "The difference between ourselves and the Navajo is that in their society institutionalized humor is not a vestigial survival but a functioning organ. Among them humor forms a recognized important adjunct of most formalized social exchange and religious performance."[48] It is unfortunate, it seems to me, that Hill did not follow the ramifications of this idea further; for if humor can be so much a part of religious exercises, it does seem hasty to class all things centrally humorous as "lay" or "secular." It would be illogical to assume that all humor among the Navajos is religious, of course, but we do need to be ready for classifications other than our own.

In the tale above, and in all other Coyote tales I have heard, one is struck by the presence both of humor and of those cultural references against which the morality of Coyote's actions may be judged. We may certainly agree with Hill that the humor does prevent a lag in interest, but far beyond that it functions as a way of directing the responses of the audience vis-à-vis significant moral factors. Causing children to laugh at an action because it is thought to be weak, stupid, or excessive is to order their moral assessment of it without recourse to open explanation or didacticism. What Hennigh says about moral reactions to Eskimo incest tales is exactly applicable here: to enjoy moral defections in a tale, "a listener must be given the opportunity to tell himself,

'I wouldn't do a thing like that.' Thus assured, he can enjoy both the vicarious pleasure of witnessing a tabu being broken and the direct pleasure of moral superiority."[49] Why, though, would one want to feel superior to someone who functions like a deity? What is there about Coyote in particular that he can be both the powerful force he is and the butt of humor in these tales?

First of all, the Navajos did not invent Coyote, as we all know; he is a common character in the tales of many American Indian tribes. Also, as Paul Radin and others have shown, there is something psychologically compelling about Trickster figures that seems to work beyond the local plot structure of any particular Trickster story. These matters have been dealt with amply by others, and I do not propose to open up those topics again here. The real question is that of how the Coyote stories function within the Navajo view of things in addition to, or in spite of, the universal traits treated by comparatists.

It is important to know that the central Navajo religious ideas are concerned with health and order; very likely, to the Navajo mind, these two concepts are in fact inseparable. Moreover, the kind of order conceived of is one primarily of ritual order, that is, order imposed by human religious action; and, for the Navajos, this is largely a matter of creating and maintaining health. Health, on its part, is seen as stretching far beyond the individual: it concerns his whole people as well as himself, and it is based in large part on a reciprocal relationship with the world of nature, mediated through ritual.[50] The world is seen as an essentially disordered place which may bring to man at any time bad dreams, witches, encounters with unhealthy animals and situations (lightning, ants), and all sorts of unnamed hazards. Man himself may run afoul of nature by not being under control; that is, his own natural desires, if allowed full rein, can cause disease (the best example is, of course, excess of any sort). In fact, one common way of envisioning evil among the Navajos is to describe it as the absence of order, or as something which is ritually not under control.[51] Man, in other words, uses his rituals to establish an island (the Navajos might call it a "world") of stability and health in what is essentially—to his view—an unpredictable universe. Man's ability to survive culturally is related directly to his ability to impose the resources of his mind, ritually directed, on an otherwise chaotic scene. Nature, of course, is distracting, and in its way fights against regularization. In the myths and stories one finds continual evidence that the concepts of order are continually being challenged (and thereby authenticated in importance) by exponents of that Nature which exists outside man. Hill, for example, quoting Washington Matthews's earlier account, discusses the clown's antics during the Night Chant: "Thus with acts of buffoonery does he endeavor to relieve the tedium of the monotonous performance of the night. . . . His exits and entrances are often erratic."[52] What he does not mention (and appears not to have known) is that the Night Chant uses what we might call monotony to establish order, and full attention to the entire proceedings is of considerable importance; as with the other rituals, the efficacy of the ceremony is seen as lying in direct proportion to the attention of the participants (which include even the onlookers). Missing a part brings about weakness in the whole. As Gladys Reichard points out of the Night Chant, even within the myth itself inattention to ritual details is dramatically denounced.[53] The clown, then, as far as the serious participant is concerned, does not play the part of a comic reliever but acts as a test, a challenge to order, a living representative of that full world of good *and* evil which exists around us.

I think the position of Coyote in the tales I have been discussing here is roughly analogous to this kind of challenge. If Coyote really were, as Reichard suggests, the exponent of irresponsibility, lust, and lack of control, his continued central role in moral stories would be puzzling, except, as noted above, for purposes of establishing a sense of moral superiority. But certainly one could feel even more easily superior to a nondeity if that were all there is to the matter. And why would a deity be, as Reichard describes him: "sneaking, skulking, shrewd, tricky, mischievous, provoking, exasperating, contrary, undependable, amusing, cowardly, obstinate, disloyal, dishonest, lascivious, sacreligious," to quote a few?[54] Indeed, in her view, Coyote seems almost the demonic opposite of a white Boy Scout (or of a white God, for that matter).

For whatever it is worth, Yellowman sees Coyote as an important entity in his religious views precisely because he is not ordered. He, unlike all others, experiences everything; he is, in brief, the exponent of all possibilities. Putting this together with Yellowman's comments, mentioned above, that Coyote makes it possible for things to happen (or for man to envision the possibility of certain things occurring), it seems to me that Coyote functions in the oral literature as a symbol of that chaotic Everything within which man's rituals have created an order for survival. Mankind limits (sometimes severely) participation in everything, but remains responsive to the exercise of moral judgment on all things. Mankind, in ordering life, thus uses certain devices to help conceive of order—in this case stories which dramatize the absence of it. The Coyote materials, then, may be seen as ways of conceptualizing, of forming models of those abstractions which are at the heart of Navajo religion.

It is not off the subject, I hope, to mention that when I lived with Yellowman's family in Montezuma Canyon, I once came down with what appears to have been pneumonia and was diagnosed by a Navajo practitioner as one in need of the Red Ant ceremony. A medicine man (in Navajo, literally, a "singer") was sent for who knew the ceremony, and I was later advised I was being treated for red ants in my system which I had no doubt picked up by urinating on an anthill. Some time after the ritual, which was quite successful I must point out, I had occasion to discuss the treatment with the singer: Had I really had ants in my system, did he think? His answer was a hesitant "no, not ants, but Ants" (my capitalization, to indicate the gist of his remark). Finally, he said, "We have to have a way of thinking strongly about disease." I now take this to be a ritual counterpart of the functions I have described above in the Coyote materials. As ways of thinking and ordering they seem consciously symbolic (but not the less "real" to the users) and much more akin to what I would call artistic modes of thought than they are to anything we can classify by our normal concepts of genre. At least they are not the simple tales of amusement that so many have taken them for in the past. It would seem difficult indeed to remove them from the total context of Navajo religious thought.

II. The 1979 (Winter) Translation

In this line-by-line translation we have tried to come as close as possible to Yellowman's narration while keeping the meaning clear in English. We have endeavored to present each meaningful unit of thought and expression as spoken by the narrator, using his own pauses and phrasing as guides for the lines and verses and reproducing where possible particularized narrational devices indicating stress, subordination, parallelism, and parenthesis.

Format

Since Navajo is itself a tonal language, the device of multilevel print used by Tedlock for Zuni translations seems inapplicable for indicating stylistic elements of Navajo. Hymes has pointed out, further, that pauses, in and of themselves, may not be clear markers of structural units (like stanzas and verses).[55] We concur in that reservation and use pauses here only as convenient ways to group utterances and keep track of them as units of expression. We leave aside for the time being the important task of determining whether there are particular and linguistic features which might show these "verses" to have deeper structural or textural foundation. Thus, the main units of meaning are here represented as "scenes," larger groupings of actions related to main actors in the story, carried out in specific locales, as will be shown below.

Within scenes, lines are grouped by the pacing provided by the narrator. Compared to other possibilities (topic, grammar, and so on), this seemed to be a less arbitrary way of dividing the piece into coherent sets of lines, for pacing and intonation are obviously important and carefully articulated elements of style for Yellowman even though his pauses do not constitute neat boundaries for solid stanzaic definition (for example, some pauses fall in the middle of ideas). A move from one line to the next, along the left margin, indicates the completion of a thought or phrase as indicated by the narrator's pacing. Utterances too long for presentation in one line are carried over in indented lines following; where possible, these indented lines also indicate subordinated or parallel or explanatory elements where such placement matches the mood of the utterance. Longer pauses than those between lines (usually less than one second) are used to group lines into "verses"; the duration of these pauses is shown in seconds between the lines. Verses are numbered from beginning to end; scenes are designated by capital letters.

On the right margin appear sparse but important references

to narrator style and audience response. Not much detail is given because these matters are already discussed in the earlier article. References to the narrator are in italics and in brackets; descriptions of audience response are in italics only.

Vocabulary

Several words are retained in Navajo because of their special function. Ma'i as a personage in the story is more important than any biological considerations about coyotes as animals, just as Hamlet as a personage in the play is more important than the corporeal being or the life and daily affairs of the person who plays the role. The main difference between Ma'i and Hamlet—in this regard—is that Euro-American audiences are said to *suspend disbelief* in watching a play, while Navajos can be said to *intensify their sense of reality* by watching Ma'i.

Although Skunk is not as powerful or ubiquitous a mythic figure as Ma'i, we retain his Navajo name (Golizhi) so that both main characters can have analogous reference in the narrative. The term *shińa'ash* is retained because of the pointed humorous irony of its usage; surely the implications of trust, kinship, and interdependence in its translation—"one who walks with me"— are undercut by Ma'i's use of it in reference to someone he is about to manipulate, cheat, and deprive of food.

Markers

The phrase *jiní* "it is said," turns out to be far more heavily used in this rendition of the story than Barre Toelken had earlier thought. Indeed, having encountered it as an apologetic device in some conversations, Toelken offered the confident assurance in the notes to the earlier translation that while one of Edward Sapir and Harry Hoijer's informants had used *jiní* thirty-nine times in a brief version of this story, Yellowman hardly used it at all when narrating directly to his family. On the contrary, the term is used in this text thirty-four times, usually in a contracted form often uttered in a near whisper (*jn*) and thus easy to miss. Believing it was not there, Toelken did not hear it. It occurs most heavily in sections of the story where description is central, least heavily where dramatic dialogue between two characters is taking place.

An important element of meaning totally left out of consideration in the first translation is the intensifier *hááhgóóshį́*. It can be translated in some positions as "very," but most often here it appears before or after a line to establish a sense of importance, intensity of action, urgency, acceleration, or stress for the whole idea. It is the oral equivalent of italics, or of several exclamation points. Although it appears as a word in Navajo, its effect is rhetorical and stylistic. To retain its function without throwing it in as a long Navajo word to confuse matters, we have opted for a symbolic representation: [!!!]. Some speculations on the use of this device will be offered below in the critical conclusion. Here it is important to note that the word sounds very much like *hágoshį́* ("okay," "all right") or like *ákoshi* ("and so then"), especially to non-Navajo ears, and particularly when the narrator contracts it to something like *haowshį*, and delivers it in a softer voice than that used for surrounding action words. Toelken subordinated it (and overlooked it in many cases) in the belief that it was a personal redundancy of Yellowman—in the nature of "you know?" in contemporary American English. Thus its role as a means of foregrounding certain key actions remained undiscovered and undiscussed in the earlier translation [!!!], even though style and texture were the intended subjects of the essay.

Another Navajo device lets the reader know that parenthetical explanation or observation is being presented (as in verse 17, where a name for a plant is immediately defined right in the midst of action). Where parentheses appear in the text, they represent Yellowman's formulaic variation in volume and pitch. Brackets in the text, on the other hand, are our device for registering any understood implications or any features of grammar where the total meaning is not susceptible to translation. For example, Navajo has a term for dancing which defines both the shape and motion of the dance and the way people join in; verse 33 shows an attempt to capture it in brackets, but still missing is the movement implied, a regular surging around in unison.

Word order

Word order, if followed exactly, would make the translation almost totally incomprehensible. Even so, where possible we have retained something very close to the original. Terms like "he said" and "they say" are used in exactly the same position, for example. For another, note that the first line of verse 38 starts with a reference to urine, as does the Navajo text, for the stress is clearly on the discomfiture caused by Golishi's scent, and the mention of urine early in the line maintains the foregrounding of the original. Other attempts are a bit more awkward: verses 30, 31, and 32 try to show the Navajo capacity for combining actions of different kinds, in this case running out and back and reporting on a condition while in transit. The only comfort here is that it's even more awkward in "standard" English description: "The jackrabbit ran over there and ran back, and during his return run reported excitedly that it was true." Given the choice, we took nonstandard awkwardness over standard constipation, an attitude which clearly would have benefited the prose translation had it been more bravely applied.

Overview of scenes and verses

Just as *King Lear* is not to be described simply as "how a man found out that things are not what they seem," just as *Beowulf* is not "a story about how a young man grew up to be king," so this story cannot fairly be described as a story about "how Coyote tricked Skunk and the prairie dogs and was tricked in return." As the essay attached to the prose translation demonstrates, the story provides important models of world view and morality, and in its evocative texture suggests attitudes and evaluative perspectives on important abstractions of life which relate to health, stability, and order. These concerns do not simply float up out of an uncomplicated plot structure; rather, they cluster in tableau scenes in which particular actors are shown in particular actions in particular places. Following the lead of Melville Jacobs and the applied examples of Hymes, we feel these clusterings can—indeed must—be taken in the nature of scenes or acts in a play: as intentional dramatic interactions played out intentionally on a meaningful stage. These scenes have the effect of spatial or gestural metaphors excited in the minds of the listeners by hearing the particulars "assembled" by a skilled narrator (rather than by watching the assemblage on a stage).

These clusterings are distilled in setting and action, and do not utilize the lineal development in plot which we would normally associate with an "act" in drama; for this reason, we have labeled them "scenes." The opening scene, A, combines a formulaic line (*Ma'i joldloshi lá eeyá*) with a statement which ties Ma'i to a particular landscape and with the narrator's remembrance of *Dinetah*, "Navajo country." The closing formula, I, is not a scene in this same spatial or geographic sense, but is a rhetorical reference to the cultural setting in which the tale is known and in which it has just been heard and understood. It could as easily be translated, "That's how it happened, they (i.e., we) say."

Broken out separately in terms of actor, principal actions, setting, and moral import, the scenes may be described as follows:

Scene/verse		actor(s)	action(s)	setting	moral topic
A	1–2	Ma'i	trotting	Where-the-Wood-Floats-Out	open; potential for recklessness
B	3–17	Ma'i, prairie dogs	running, planning	desert; prairie dog village	anger
C	18–26	Ma'i, Golizhi	running, planning	clump of plants, near water	deception
D	27–32	Golizhi, small animals	running, confirming	prairie dog village; dance	deception
E	33–40	Golizhi, small animals	dancing, urinating, killing	Ma'i's "body"	deception, desecration of the dead
F	41–46	Ma'i, Golizhi	cooking, running, jumping	prairie dogs' bake pit	competition, deception
G	47–58	Ma'i, Golizhi	running, digging	cooking pit; race "offstage"	arrogance, selfishness, frustration, desecration of ritual
H	59–62	Ma'i, Golizhi	pacing, begging	Golizhi elevated, Ma'i below	discovery
I	63	narrator	recalling	home	participation in culture

Note that each scene begins with a move toward focus on the particulars of actors, action, and setting while recalling details of the previous scene. These transitional markers (B3, C18, D27, E33, F41, G47, H59) are clear indications of meaningful groupings in the mind of the narrator, and of course they function as powerful directions for the imaginations of the listeners. Moreover, these boundary markers are distinctly different from the continuation-summary device used by Yellowman at the beginning of verse 35, where he takes up the story again after having interrupted his narration for a brief rest. The styles of these two kinds of passages are so different yet so closely related to the "direction" of the narration that they can hardly be coincidental.

Topical connections

There is a relationship for the Navajos between prairie dogs and rain, probably because the prairie dogs live underground and thus represent the "other side," the reciprocal responses of earth and her inhabitants to those forces that move from the essentially male sky. Similarly, the Hopis connect snakes with lightning and rain; the idea is wholeness, totality: it is not to be shrugged off as erroneous science, but experienced as accurate sacred engagement. In one area of the reservation, when a rodent control program was proposed by the government in the thirties or forties, the local Navajos complained, "If you kill the prairie dogs, who will there be to cry for rain?" When older Navajos talk about "the good old days" (that is, before the whites came), they say, "There were prairie dogs all over this area."

Rain relates to fertility (Navajos have a vivid and live sense of this, even distinguishing clearly between Male and Female rain) and thus to food, which is of course a strong central concern in this story. Much of the early part of the story is associated with water (the locale's name, the rain storm, the flood, Golizhi's trip to fetch water); but after Ma'i and Golizhi conspire to deceive and kill the small animals, there is no more mention of water, and Ma'i winds up not with a feast, but with only a few bones to gnaw on.

Dances are usually associated with ceremonials which maintain, insure, or restore health, stability, soundness, and "Beauty";

one would not normally think of dancing in celebration of some-one's death unless one wanted to suggest the dark and evil side of life encompassed by witchcraft. Neither would one play dead and portray his own flesh as decaying: it would be the direct gestural enactment of everything opposite and counter to the Navajo way of health and long life.

Betrayals and outright lying are frowned upon although one often encounters them in jokes and tricks. Playing jokes on people is a common pastime among the Navajos, so the logic of pretend-ing in this story is of course deliciously funny to a Navajo audi-ence. But jokes of this sort? Jokes that end in competition for food instead of reciprocation, that end in death, that feature a betrayal of one's partner? These jokes are very much in the cate-gory of traveling salesman jokes for Anglo-Americans, for they encapsulate exactly those actions which are *not* supposed to take place in real life, actions which cause us anxiety even to think about. The narrative provides us, among other things, with a way of projecting and experiencing our anxieties. To Navajos, serious and repeated lying, extreme irritability, impatience, open frustra-tion, compulsive competition, and breaking of taboos are all seen as symptomatic of illness, and illness is a big concern for everyone nearby. In brief, nearly every action in this story, seen in its moral frame, is "wrong," in a traditional sense, even though within the narrative frame each action has its own internal logic, especially given the well-known unpredictable aspect of Ma'i's personality.

A   (1)   Ma'i was trotting along [having always done so] .   [*slowly*]
-4-

     (2)   At a place I'm not familiar with called "Where the Wood Floats
          Out" he was walking along, it is said.
-4-

B   (3)   Then, also in an open area, it is said [!!!] ,
          he was walking along in the midst of many prairie dogs [!!!] .
-1-

     (4)   [!!!] The prairie dogs were cursing him, it is said [!!!] ,
          all crowded together, yelling.
-1-

     (5)   He went along further into their midst.
-1-

     (6)   Then he walked further.
-3-

(7)   [!!!] He got angry and soon began to feel hostile.

-2-

(8)   After a while it was noon.

-1-

(9)   He wanted [implied: looking upward] a cloud   *[slower, nasal]*
        to appear
    (His reason was that he started hating the prairie dogs),
        so he asked for rain.

-2-   *smiles, quiet laughter*

(10)   Then a cloud appeared, it is said.
     "If it would only rain on me," he said.   *smiles, heavy breathing*
     And that's what happened, it is said.

-2-

(11)   "If only there could be rain in my footprints."
     And that's what happened, it is said.
     "If only water would ooze up between my toes
       as I walk along," he said.

-3-   *open amusement*

(12)   Then everything happened as he said, it is said.

-4-   *[clears throat]*

(13)   "If only the water would come up to my knees," he said.
     And that's what happened.

-2-

(14)   "If only the water would be up to my back
       so that only my ears would be out of the water."   *[nasal]*

-13-   *heavy breathing; baby cries*

(15)   "If I could only float," he said.   *[nasal]*
     Then, starting to float,
     "Where the prairie dogs are,
       if I could only land there," he said.

-3-   *quiet laughter*

(16)   He came to rest in the midst of the prairie dog town, it is said.

-3-

(17)   Someplace in the *diz—*   *smiles, quiet laughter*
     (*diz* is the name of a plant that grows in clumps)—
     he landed [implied: along with other debris] hung up
     in the clump, it is said.

-4-   *quiet laughter*

C (18)   And there he was lying after the rain.
     And then Golizhi was running by to fetch water.   *[slower]*
       (Ma'i was pretending to be dead)   *smiles exchanged*
     Then he [Golizhi] was running.   *glances*
     He [Ma'i] called out to him, it is said.
     "Come here," he said, and Golizhi came to him,   *[very nasal]*
     it is said.

-6-   *suppressed giggling*

(19) "Shiłna'ash," he said [very seriously].   [*nasal*]

-2-   *quiet laughter, expelling air*

(20) "'The hated one has died, and has washed up   [*nasal*]
          where the prairie dogs are,' tell them that, shiłna'ash."

-3-

(21) "'He's already got maggots,' you tell them," he said.   [*nasal*]

-2-

(22) "Slendergrass, it is called—shake that Slendergrass
          so the seeds fall off.
      In my crotch, in my nose, in the back part of my mouth,
          scatter some around, then put some inside my ears," he said.
      "'He's got maggots,' you tell them.   *quiet laughter*
      'The hated one has been washed out.'"

-3-   *quiet laughter*

(23) "Make four clubs and put them under me.

-3-

(24) 'We'll dance over him.
      We're all going to meet over there,'
          you tell them," he said.

-1-

(25) "This is how," he said.
      . . . . [wording indistinct] . . . .
      . . . . "dancing around" . . .
      [implied: Golizhi is to join in these actions]
      . . . "'Hit Ma'i in the ribs'" . . . .   *breathing*

-1-

(26) "Be careful not to hit me too hard!
      'Slowly, gently, like this,'   *laughter*
          you tell them," he said.

-5-   [*clears throat*]

D (27) This happened.   [*normal tone*]
      He ran home, and gave out the word to the prairie dogs, it is said.
      "The hated one is washed out [!!!]."

-2-

(28) There were rabbits and other animals [there],
          and even groundsquirrels.
      (Those animals which are food for him were gathered [!!!])
      [!!!] Now the people were dancing, it is said, at the meeting.

-3-

(29) First, he [Golizhi] said, "It's true! It's true!   [*tones exaggerated*]
      Let's have one of you who runs fast run over there to find out."

-1-

(30) Then Jackrabbit ran and, "It's true!" said,   *quiet giggling*
          running back, it is said.

-1-

(31) Then Cottontail ran and, "It's true!" said,
running back, it is said.

-1-

(32) Then Prairiedog ran and, they say, "It's true!" said,
running back, it is said.

-1-

E (33) At that time there was a big gathering [!!!].
They were dancing,[implied: couples periodically stepping into circle]
it is said.
Whatever they were singing, I don't know.

-2-

(34) "The hated one is dead," they were saying [!!!];
the club is beside him; they were hitting
him in the ribs, it is said.   [*delivered in one long breath*]
-rest-   *expelling of air*
— [*narrator rests for about five minutes, drinks coffee*] —

(35) Then they continued with what they were doing,
and more and more people came.
Then Golizhi-ye-ne said (remembering Ma'i's plan)
"You are all dancing;
While you are looking up, while you are saying,
you say 'Dance in that manner,' you tell them [!!!]
while you're in charge there, shiłna'ash," he said.

-2-

(36) Then they were dancing.
Then, "Waay, waay up there a *t'aadziłgai* is running through the
air," he said,
Golizhi said.   *one girl: hn!*

-1-

(37) Then, when they were all looking up,
he urinated upward
so that it fell in their eyes, the urine.
-3-   *open laughter*

(38) His urine the animals were rubbing from their eyes [!!!].
"'The one who is hated is dead?'" he [Ma'i] said, jumping up [!!!].
-1-   *laughter, giggling*

(39) He grabbed the clubs from under him [!!!].
-3-   *laughter, giggling*

(40) He used the clubs on them [all in a row, in one circular swing].
They were all clubbed to death.   [*laughter*]
-8-   *laughter*

F (41)   Then,
        "Let us cook by burying, shiłna'ash," he said.
        "Dig right here," he said [!!!].
        And he dug a trench, Golizhi did.
                        -2-

(42)   After he dug a ditch, he built a fire.
        He put the food into the pit.
        Then he [Ma'i] thought of something new.
                        -1-

(43)   "Let's have a foot race, shiłna'ash.
        Whoever comes back first,
                this will be his," he said.   *light laughter*
        "No," he [Golizhi] said, but he [Ma'i] won the argument.
        "I can't run fast," he [Golizhi] said.
        "While I stay here, you start loping," he [Ma'i] said.
                        -1-

(44)   ... [indistinct] ... while Ma'i pretended to do something
                to his ankles, he [Golizhi] started to run,
        then, over the hill he ran,
             and ran into an abandoned hole.
                        -2-

(45)   In a little while, he [Ma'i] suddenly spurted away.
                        -3-

(46)   A torch he tied to his tail
        and the smoke was pouring out behind him
                as he ran.   *[laughter]*
                    -17-   *laughter*

G (47)   While he was running over there,
        Golizhi ran back, it is said,
                there where he had buried the food [!!!].
        He dug them up and took them up into the rocks,
                it is said.   *amusement*
        Four little prairie dogs he reburied,
        then he was sitting back up there, it is said.
        [!!!] Ma'i ran back, it is said,   *light laughter*
                back to the place where the prairie dogs were buried.
        He leaped over it.   *[laughter]*
                    -4-   *increased laughter*

(48)   "Hwah!" he said.   *[laughter]*
                    -8-   *extended laughter*

(49)   "Shiłna'ash—I wonder how far back he's plodding,
                Mr. His-Urine," he said.

-6- *loud laughter*

(50) [!!!] Sighing, he lay down,
     pretended to lie down, in the shade.
     He jumped up and leaped over to the pit. [*laughter*]
     -1- *laughter*

(51) He thrust a pointed object into the ground
     and grabbed the tail of the prairie dog first, it is said.
     Only the tail came loose. [*chuckle*]
     -1- *light laughter*

(52) "Oh no! the fire has gotten to the tail," he said.
     -2- *loud laughter*

(53) So he grabbed the stick and thrust it into the ground again;
     a little prairie dog he dug up, it is said.
     "I'm not going to eat this [meat]," he said,
     and he flung it away toward the east.
     -2- *light laughter*

(54) He thrust it into the ground again; [*slower*]
     a little prairie dog he dug up.
     "I'm not going to eat this," he said,
     and he flung it away toward the south.
     -2- *light laughter*

(55) He thrust it into the ground again; [*slower*]
     a little prairie dog he dug up.
     "I'm not going to eat this," he said,
     and he flung it away toward the west.
     -2- *breathing*

(56) He thrust it into the ground again; [*sleepily*]
     a little prairie dog he dug up.
     "I'm not going to eat this," he said,
     and he flung it away toward the north.
     -1- *breathing*

(57) He thrust repeatedly in many places, it is said,
     and couldn't find any.
     Nothing, it is said.
     There weren't any, it is said.
     -2- *expelling breath*

(58) He couldn't, he walked [frustrated] around in circles.
     He went around and he picked up those little prairie dogs he had
       thrown away.
     Then he picked up every little bit
       and ate it all.
     -2- *quiet laughter*

H (59) Then he started to follow [Golizhi's] tracks, it is said, *amusement*
            but he couldn't pick up the trail.
        He kept following the tracks, back and forth,
            to where the rock meets the sand.   *boy: hn!*
        (He didn't bother to look up.)
                            -2-
(60)   He [Golizhi] dropped a bone and he [Ma'i] looked up, it is said.
        It dropped at his feet.
                            -1-   *quiet laughter*
(61)   "Shitna'ash, share with me again
        [implied: what I shared with you previously."]   [*brief laughter*]
                            -5-   *brief laughter*
(62)   "Certainly not," he said to him, it is said.   [*slowly, seriously*]
        He was begging, to no avail, it is said.
        Golizhi kept dropping bones down to him.
        He chewed the bones, it is said.
                            -4-   *small burst of quiet laughter*
I (63)   That's how it happened, it is said.

III. Comments, Notes, Comparisons

General

For the cultural "meaning" and function of the story, see the text
and notes of the prose version. Following are some particular
ideas that have come forth from the new translation. Many of
these matters are implied or rationalized in the explanations for
the prose text, but here they have had to be dealt with head-on.
Where considerable discrepancies (real or apparent) exist between
the two versions, some accounting will be given for the difference.

Several stylistic elements are found throughout. For one
thing, pronouns referring to Ma'i and Golizhi are those normally
used in reference to human persons, not animals. Similarly,
reference to body parts is often in the form of human anatomy, as
in verse 11, where "toes" does not denote animal paws. Again, in
verse 28, "people" or "folks" is the best rendering of the collective term for the dancing animals—not the term one would normally use to denote something like a herd or pack or troop of animals.
All of these suggest little differentiation between humans and

animals in the Ma'i stories, and it is for several reasons. For one thing, the story is framed in a mythic dimension in which all possibilities are inherent, and thus factual division on physiological, biological bases (which the Navajos are keenly aware of and articulate about) is pointless. Also, as noted in the earlier article, these stories are told more to suggest a set of ethics for humans than to provide an explanation for, or exposition of, animal physiology and behavior. Referring to animals in human terms perhaps makes the abstract connections more realizable.

Another important stylistic element is Yellowman's use of a nasal, slow delivery for Ma'i's speech. The marginal notes indicate lines in which this is particularly marked, but it is necessary to remember that the style is used throughout. It is widely found in the narration of Coyote tales, and listeners look forward to its familiar tone, which is considered distinctive to the genre. So pleasant and humorous are its effects on auditors that Coyote tales without it are almost unthinkable; its presence is one dimension of the "pretty languages," the special vocabulary of beautiful ideas and textures which, in the Navajo view, are reflections of stability and order in the world (quite in contradistinction to the unstable actions of Coyote, for whose odd personality this textural network of sound acts as an ironic counterpoint).

The central actions in each scene are noticeably energetic: trotting, running, dancing, jumping, throwing. It is worth recalling that movement itself is central to Navajo thought, language, and world view. Movement is the normal condition of life. One way to intensify this idea, of course is to accelerate it, to keep the pace worked up. It is only late in the story, after Ma'i has leaped over the cooking pit so arrogantly, and has so foolishly thrown away his food, that the pace slackens to something "normal." The final scene, a tableau in which the would-be manipulator must beg for scraps from someone above him, is the only scene in which rapid movement does not take place. The pace of moral discovery and comeuppance is that of everyday life. Aggression, competition, selfishness, arrogance are out of proportion to regular movement.

Scene A

The opening is formulaic, standardized. It suggests both a particular place in Navajo country and a concept of continuity and movement in mythic reality. Ma'i has always been in motion and always will be. The phrasing suggests that we, in our present time frame, are breaking into something that has been happening continuously from out of the past, something like opening a play or a movie in medias res: "As we join the story we find . . ." We are looking through a narrative window, so to speak, at another dimension of life in which actions are always in progress. Further, the term *joldloshi* is used only of Ma'i in the Coyote tales. Normally, an animal trotting would be described as *yildlosh*; here the *jol* is distinctive of Ma'i's mythic trotting—which is always pregnant with meaning—and the suffix -*i* implies recklessness, abandon. The first line, then, *Ma'i joldloshi lá eeyá,* in which *lá* suggests past action and *eeyá* suggests the present, encapsulates a rich and complicated set of postulates within which the rest of the story has expanded meaning.

The original translation mentions a once forested area, inferred from the desert setting and the depiction of wood floating away. This is probably unwarranted, after all; at least it is irrelevant.

Scene B

Both the "I wish" of the prose translation and the "If it would only" of the poetic rendering are awkward and superficially simple-sounding attempts to represent the Navajo subjunctive, in which speaking about something is a way of projecting its real possibility. It relates to much of ritual language, in which the condition of the patient is spoken about and chanted over, in which a stable world of *reality* is created through the use of key words. Thus, while the subjunctive in European languages has the connotation of wishful thinking, or even make-believe, in Navajo it has the feel of creation. In the case of Ma'i, moreover, the audience knows from other mythic stories that control of the rains was given to him in earlier negotiations with the Holy Persons. His speaking of rain thus starts the story on a note of natural response and fertility, certainly an ironic setting against which to view his angry and selfish move toward impoverishment and hunger.

The thirteen-second pause between verses 14 and 15 is not rhetorical but circumstantial. A baby held by Yellowman wet its diapers (and Yellowman's leg), began to cry, and was handed over to its mother.

Scene C

Some serious discrepancies between translations can be seen in the interchange between Ma'i and Golizhi (verse 18). "Skunk didn't know he was there," and "Skunk turned around in fright," are simply not in the original narration and may have been inserted in the earlier translation as ways of making the scene more palpable to English readers. Further, Ma'i does not call to Golizhi four times; apparently Toelken mistook a sound in the term *bididį́į́nil* ("you tell them") for *dį́į́'* ("four"). "Skunk had a dipper" is not specifically stated in translatable form, but the idea is clearly to be inferred, since the Navajo term for fetching water is not the same as for simply going to the water to drink it there (note also the human aspect of bringing water home). Obviously, a container is involved.

Scenes C and D

Verses 20–26 and 27 reveal the original narration of Ma'i's plan and Golizhi's willing application of it. The prose translation expanded on the meaning of the plan and reported it as repeated in essence by Golizhi in the small animals' village. Actually, while the details seem parsimonious in the new direct translation, the scene is far richer than may first appear to be the case. Ma'i here talks about himself in the third person, as if to embody others' views of him; when Golizhi transmits this statement to the prairie dogs, we are told he "gave out the word," which in Navajo is something like bringing all the news. That is, we are to assume that Golizhi's disclosure is a complete recapitulation of those details outlined by Ma'i as a way of deceiving the small animals. This is now followed by an extended use of "It's true!" along with attempts by the animals to verify Ma'i's death, providing not only the irony of deception going undetected in the midst of declarations of truth, but suggesting now that their own blindness may be involved in the animals' demise.

Scene E

In verse 33 the dance is described very distinctly in Navajo: its direction is circular, the dancers are moving around in unison surges or waves, and the couples joining are stepping in at these periodic moments of movement. The regularity, the periodicity, the circularity, are all aspects of beauty, *hózhǫ́*: they are some of the cultural referents of what Helen Yellowman called "those pretty languages."

The suffix *-ye-ne* on Golizhi's name in verse 35 means that the person so called is dead, or cursed. Here it indicates the narrator's dislike for him (or at least for the role he plays here in deception). In verse 35, Golizhi rehearses to himself the specific directions given to him previously by Ma'i; thus "he" in the last line obviously refers to Ma'i.

In verse 36, Golizhi clearly calls the prairie dogs' attention to the bird (whose name here might mean "white under the wings while overhead") only once, not four times as given in the first translation. Apparently Toelken misheard *déé'* ("from") for *dįį'* ("four").

In verse 38, Ma'i jumps up and pretends (?) anger that the prairie dogs should call him dead. In English it might read, "Oh, so you say I'm dead, do you?" or "'The hated one is dead,' is he?"

Scene F

Note the dropping of proper names to a minimum during the cooking and race scenes. The audience knows very well who is who, and the pronoun "he" is not here productive of confusion.

In verse 43, instead of "Ma'i insisted"—as in the prose translation—note that he simply uses the tactic of going ahead with his plan regardless of Golizhi's objections. The effect is the same; but as is the case with most of this story, the event should be perceived as action, not as indirect description of attitude.

The rather long pause after verse 46 is no doubt due to some conversation which arose among a couple of visitors. It was quiet and unobtrusive (and the visitors could not understand the story narration anyhow), but it probably constituted a brief distraction. On the tape the narration continues about four seconds after the conversation dies down.

Ma'i's rapid return to the cooking pit (verse 47) is described in the prose translation as an attempt to "make a good finish."

This is partly supported by the [!!!] which precedes the utterance; more obvious is the fact that instead of stopping, under control, Ma'i leaps right over the spot. It's overacted, in other words; Scott calls it "obvious arrogance."

Scene G

After Ma'i's return run he rests briefly, then leaps over to the cooking pit. Tying this in with "pretended to lie down" and his later pacing back and forth, Toelken earlier understood the movement as an attempt to show how long he had waited for Golizhi before impatiently digging up the cooked prairie dogs. Scott feels rather that the present translation justifies a stress only on Ma'i's impatience and selfishness. He makes little pretense at waiting, but jumps directly toward what he thinks will be a banquet. Although he has won (he thinks) and can therefore claim the prairie dogs, Navajo custom would have him distribute shares to those who are in subordinate or associate status.

Verses 53–56 show the actual wording of the exhumation scene. One by one, in nearly exact repetition, Ma'i digs up the prairie dogs and flings them toward the cardinal directions *in ritual order*, starting in the east and continuing in a "sunwise" direction just as Navajo ceremonial movements are organized. Since his aim is selfish and his actions wasteful, however, this constitutes at least a perversion of ritual, a desecration of sacred order by subordinating it to personal appetites. The original translation reduces the redundancy by collapsing these important actions too far.

A similar reduction of meaning is found in the passage represented by verse 57: the prose translation gives no sense of the repeated or intensified negative results of Ma'i's digging in various places. It is important because of its relation to Ma'i's frustration in the next verse (58), the sense of which is totally missing from the earlier text. Yellowman does not stumble here; he intentionally words the line "He couldn't, he walked around," in such a way as to express the way in which Ma'i's walking is a measure of his inability to find what he "knows" is there. Instead of saying, "Ma'i was frustrated," Yellowman narrates a scene of frustration, using phrasing which suggests a mental impasse.

IV. Conclusions

The use of *hááshgóóshįį́* ([!!!]), totally missed in the first translation, begs for comment but defies full analysis. Clearly it is used in very important passages (but not in every key passage, it would seem). In six instances it appears in lines that concern large gatherings of animals (B3, B4, D28 [twice], E33, E34); the open area as setting is stressed (B3); in D27 and E34 the lie that "The hated one is washed out," is spoken, first by Golizhi, then by the crowd; Ma'i's instructions to Golizhi about the deceptive dance are stressed (E35); Ma'i's sudden "resurrection" and use of his clubs are foregrounded (E38, E39); Ma'i's ordering of Golizhi to dig in a particular spot is stressed (F41), as is the return of both animals from the race (G47); finally, Ma'i's pretended wait (G50) is underlined. Are these key elements of cultural reference, being foregrounded for some special reason? Are they simply aspects of Yellowman's presentation, allowing for the building of particularly vivid or intensified scenes (other scenes being intensified by still other devices such as pacing, intonations, ritual inferences, and so on)? The latter is more likely the case, but a demonstration of it would require an equally detailed look at several other stories told by the same narrator *and* a survey of other orally delivered stories by other Navajo raconteurs. We have decided to be prudent and not try to eat all the prairie dogs at once.

One final comment on meaning seems appropriate after all the detail of this scrutiny. In the original article, Toelken held that the real cultural meaning of the tale resided not in its structure but in its texture. This was stated so baldly for two reasons: first, accounting for the details of plot structure seemed to elucidate so few of those elements which were clearly of importance to the Navajos, and seemed in fact to do no more than solidify the stereotype of Indian literature as childlike, simple, uncomplicated (read: unworthy of notice by serious scholars of "real" literature); second, it was meant as a direct statement to those who were at the time classifying and studying nearly everything in folklore in structural terms (usually *lineal* terms, at that, which covertly—and murderously—subordinate all traditional materials to the Western world view: classification, analysis, and evaluation). Toelken hoped to show that the quarry was "in another place." But as bald tactical pronouncements often turn out, this one was oversimplified, for the "meaning," really, is no more *in* the texture than it is *in* the structure. Actually both structure and texture unite to provide an excitement of meaning which already exists elsewhere, in the shared ideas and customs of people raised in an intensely traditional society. The structure provides the framework of something recognizable taking place through a brief span of time. The texture evokes emotional and philosophical attitudes, moral assessments, and ethical responses by bringing certain performance features together in such a way as to create models of, and challenges to, recognizable clusters of belief.[56] But these beliefs, attitudes, responses, and so on, are the results of long years of traditional development, experience, ritual practice, human evaluations of old ideas as they are seen in continually changing historical contexts. Thus, the stories act like "surface structure" in language: by their articulation they touch off a Navajo's deeper accumulated sense of reality; they excite perspectives on truth by bringing a "critical mass" together which is made up of ethical opposites (one thinks of the Zen *koan* here); they provide culturally enjoyable correlatives to a body of thought so complicated and profound that vicarious experience in it through entertainment is one of the only access points available to most people.[57]

We overheard a literature professor say that if only every other chapter had been deleted from *Moby Dick*, Melville might have made a decent whaling story out of it. We hope it is clear from the evidence brought forward here that the same effect may be had in Native American literature by simply presenting the text in prose and by ignoring those textural references that make it as impossible for a listener to think a story is "about an adventure of a coyote" as it is for a reader of Melville, no matter how dull, to think that *Moby Dick* is "a story about a whale."

Notes

1. See Dell Hymes, "Discovering Oral Performance and Measured Verse in American Indian Narrative," *New Literary History* 8, no. 3 (Spring 1977): 433-57; idem, "Breakthrough into Performance," in *Folklore: Performance and Communication,* ed. Dan Ben-Amos and Kenneth S. Goldstein (The Hague: Mouton, 1975), pp. 11-74; idem, "Folklore's Nature and the Sun's Myth," *Journal of American Folklore* 88, no. 350 (October–December

1975): 345-69; Dennis Tedlock, *Finding the Center: Narrative Poetry of the Zuni Indians* (New York: Dial Press, 1972); idem, "On the Translation of Style in Oral Narrative," in *Toward New Perspectives in Folklore,* ed. Américo Paredes and Richard Bauman (Austin: University of Texas Press, 1971), pp. 114-33.

2. The Sun's Myth may be found in Franz Boas, *Kathlamet Texts,* Bureau of American Ethnology Bulletin no. 26 (Washington, D.C.: GPO, 1901), pp. 26-33.

3. Prose translation and interlinear text in Franz Boas, *Tsimshian Texts,* Bureau of American Ethnology Bulletin no. 27 (Washington, D.C.: GPO, 1902), pp. 200-210; the first passage is on p. 203, the second on pp. 209-10.

4. *Genre* 2 (September 1969): 211-35; rpt. in *Folklore Genres,* ed. Dan Ben-Amos (Austin: University of Texas Press, 1976), pp. 145-70.

5. By way of only a few examples, see Gladys Reichard, *Navaho Religion* (New York: Pantheon, 1950), concordance A; Leland C. Wyman, ed., *Beautyway: A Navaho Ceremonial* (New York: Bollinger Foundation, 1957), p. 131; Leland C. Wyman, *The Red Antway of the Navaho,* Navaho Religion Series, vol. 5 (Santa Fe: Museum of Navajo Ceremonial Art, 1965); David P. McAllester, ed., *The Myth and Prayers of the Great Star Chant, and the Myth of the Coyote Chant,* Navaho Religion Series, vol. 4 (Santa Fe: Museum of Navajo Ceremonial Art, 1956), pp. 91-105; Father Berard Haile, O.F.M., and Mary C. Wheelwright, eds., *Emergence Myth,* Navaho Religion Series, vol. 3 (Santa Fe: Museum of Navajo Ceremonial Art, 1949), p. 130.

6. See note 11, below, concerning Sapir's text of the tale used in this study. [1979: the proper spelling of the term is *jiní*; the proper translation is "it is said."]

7. Perhaps it is well to explain that this adoption featured none of the Hollywood elements which might be imagined by the reader who is unfamiliar with the Navajos. Tsinaabąąs Yazhi simply announced at an evening meal that he was going to be my father and that henceforth I was probably to be known to others as Tsinaabąąs Yazhi Biyé' (Little Wagon's Son). After that point my address to him was *shizhé'é* ("my father") instead of the joking *shicheii* ("my grandfather"); my form of address to his daughter, therefore, became *shádí* ("my older sister"), and to her husband, Yellowman, *shiłna'ash* [the *ł* here is pronounced like the Welsh *ll*; that is, a voiceless lateral fricative] (lit. "one who walks with me," used with the sense of "my kinsman," "my cousin").

8. His comments have been augmented by those of his daughters, one of whom supplied me the title of this paper during a session in which Yellowman attempted to explain his choice of vocabulary in the Coyote tales. I was having difficulty with a certain phrase when Helen Yellowman interjected in English, "He just means he uses those pretty languages."

9. Melville Jacobs made this observation in his extremely valuable study, *The Content and Style of an Oral Literature: Clackamas Chinook Myths and Tales* (New York: Viking Foundation Publications in Anthropology, 1959), p. 128; but even Jacobs's title betrays the fact that our culture makes a distinction between sacred and secular which is not so clearly marked in most Indian tribes (and particularly the Navajo).

10. David F. Aberle, *The Peyote Religion among the Navaho* (Chicago: University of Chicago Press, 1966), p. 103n; Aberle notes that some people did respond to only one question, which may mean the custom is breaking down. It is difficult to determine, however, how even the occasional recourse to this custom may affect data drawn from questionnaires as they are subjected to statistical analysis.

11. Elsie Clews Parsons presented a text of it with the title "Coyote Plays Dead," in "Navaho Folk Tales," *Journal of American Folklore* 36 (October–December 1923): 371-72, and related it to a Pueblo tale of suspected Spanish origin which appeared in her earlier article, "Pueblo-Indian Folk-Tales, Probably of Spanish Provenience," *Journal of American Folklore* 31 (April–June 1918): 229-30. A very awkward native text is given in Edward Sapir and Harry Hoijer, eds., *Navaho Texts* (Iowa City, Iowa: Linguistic Society of America, 1942), pp. 20-25; entitled "Coyote Makes Rain," it employs the self-conscious *jiní* ("it is said") thirty-nine times in what appears to me a much collapsed form of the story.

12. The Navajo wording here is complex, and refers to this story as one of a series of repeated actions. The closest English equivalent that I can think of would be "in one of these episodes," but I have avoided that translation because it implies something more objectively literary than does the original. The point, however, is more than linguistic: Yellowman here limits himself to one incident in Coyote's career, but opens the narration in such a way as to remind his listeners of the whole fabric of Coyote legend. Compare the presumable effect of this on native listeners with that of Sapir's text, mentioned above (note 11), where the narrator is telling a tale to an outsider in which the first phrase translates, "Long ago Coyote was trotting along, they say."

13. Ma'i does not want to alert the prairie dogs; but in order to get the desired results, he must speak these wishes aloud. Therefore, he phrases them as if he were seeking only personal respite from the heat (Yellowman).

14. The word Yellowman uses here would normally be translated "palms"; it is one of several indications throughout the Coyote canon (and supported by Yellowman in conversation) that Coyote is not always envisioned as a coyote.

15. *Golizhi,* lit. "one whose urine stinks."

16. I retain this term for lack of a proper English equivalent, and because it is distinctive to the speech of Coyote. Meaning literally "one who walks with me," it is used familiarly among male friends in the figurative

sense of "cousin," or even something like the English "old buddy." Essentially, it is a term of trust as well as friendship or relation. Coyote uses the term constantly, especially when he is trying to put something over on someone else; thus its appearance usually creates a sense of irony, and its retention here may help signal its literary function for the English reader. As noted above (note 7), the ł is pronounced as a voiceless lateral fricative.

17. Four is the number in Navajo narrative, custom, and ritual which corresponds to three in European-American folklore. Usually the fourth position "carries the weight," and normally the narrator works up to the fourth, utilizing (as we do in "Cinderella" or "The Three Pigs") the audience's recognition of the sequence to build tension. Here, however, Yellowman condenses the sequence with this descriptive comment. It seems to me that a possible aesthetic explanation for it might be that the humor (as the laughter suggests) has been chiefly connected to the first position; the rest, being important but anticlimactic, is telescoped. I have neglected to consult Yellowman on the matter, however.

18. Lit., "slender grass," a certain variety of desert grass the heads of which look like small, twisted green worms. I have not been able to find a botanical name for it.

19. The phrase uses hatał "sing"—which usually implies a ceremony connected with healing or purifying.

20. In this discussion of "what is true" there is a predominance of the vowel sound aa, with and without nasalization. The textural ramifications of this feature will be discussed below. See also notes 25 and 27 for similar passages.

21. Annie Yellowman: "It's a special kind of bird."

22. Lit., "urine."

23. Annie Y.: Now he can have revenge because their previous insults have been made even more serious by this false claim that he is dead.

24. As usual, Ma'i cons someone else into doing the work.

25. Heavy use of ąą throughout the description of Skunk hiding and Ma'i running past; see also notes 20 and 27.

26. Yellowman: He ties the burning stick to his tail in order to show off how fast he can run. Readers familiar with Navajo lore will recognize in this scene an important motif in the story of Coyote's theft of fire.

27. There is heavy use of ąą in the exhumation scene; see notes 20 and 25.

28. Probably to avoid being burned; Ma'i avoids discomfort.

29. This is humorous in part because he has already covered the ground with his own footprints: the mark of a poor hunter, and thus subject to ridicule.

30. Emphatic: dooda hee.

31. This is Yellowman's favorite ending formula. In my references to the

narrator's change of tones and styles, I have included only those variations of importance to the present study. The reader will note that most of the highly nasalized passages occur in the speech of characters; it can be assumed here that passages which are not marked were delivered in a regular narrative tone, which for Yellowman's rendition of the Coyote stories is slightly more nasalized than normal conversation and somewhat more slowly delivered.

32. This is not a new idea, of course. Hennigh puts it in a succinct cross-cultural context which nicely demonstrates the central point. See Lawrence Hennigh, "Control of Incest in Eskimo Folktales," *Journal of American Folklore* 79, no. 312 (April–June 1966): 356–69.

33. Father Liebler, called "priest with long hair" by the Navajos, is the founder, builder, and former vicar of St. Christopher's Mission to the Navajo at Bluff, Utah. Now in "retirement," he and a small group of faithful retainers build the Hat Rock Valley Retreat Center, near Oljeto. His familiarity with Navaho language and culture is long-standing; see his "Christian Concepts and Navaho Words," *Utah Humanities Review* 13, no. 1 (Winter 1959): 169–75; and "The Social and Cultural Patterns of the Navajo Indians," *Utah Historical Quarterly* 30, no. 4 (Fall 1962): 299–325.

34. Reichard, *Navaho Religion,* p. 267, points out that such language may not actually be archaic; its special usage sets it apart, and its users might attribute its effects to archaism, but it is still in wide use and is understood by all native speakers, including children.

35. This is a literal translation of the idiom; it may also mean, "They make things simple, or easy to understand."

36. Reichard, *Navaho Religion,* has a good discussion of Navajo symbolism. My own acquaintance with the symbols themselves, especially in relation to particular rituals, is spotty enough to prevent a full evaluation of Reichard's comments, but I can say that her willingness to allow for conscious art seems quite sensible; see especially her discussion of the Navajo awareness of word as symbol, p. 267.

37. Clyde Kluckhohn and Dorothea Leighton, *The Navaho,* rev. ed. (Garden City, N.Y.: Doubleday, 1962), p. 194.

38. W. W. Hill, *Navaho Humor,* General Series in Anthropology, no. 9 (Menasha, Wis., 1943), p. 19.

39. Alan Dundes, "Texture, Text, and Context," *Southern Folklore Quarterly* 28, no. 4 (December 1964): 251–65.

40. By structure I mean the formal framework, the lineal or organized form of a traditional text. In narrative, it is that particular sequence of events that makes up the story line and plot; structure is, then, the rational design of the story. While in actual artistic practice, texture and structure are tightly interrelated, one can separate for purposes of discussion what is being said from how it is being said. It is usually on the basis of structure that definitions of genre are founded in literature.

41. Dundes, "Texture, Text, and Context," p. 254.

42. René Wellek and Austin Warren, *Theory of Literature* (New York: Harcourt, Brace & Co., 1942), pp. 235, 241, for example.

43. Northrop Frye, *Anatomy of Criticism* (New York: Atheneum, 1967), pp. 246-48.

44. Jacobs has suggested (*Content and Style,* pp. 211-19) that our conceptions of drama much more closely match the characteristics of folk "stories," for in most cases (at least in most Indian materials) a tale is not told in its entirety; rather, certain key features and actions are described in such a way as to cause the audience to envision a drama in progress. The audience creates a mental stage upon which characters manipulated by the narrator play their scenes. I suspect that this may be true of all oral "narrative," including such things as the ballads and tales of our own culture, and that our penchant for applying generic terms based on visible form to oral materials has led us constantly away from the essence we seek.

45. See notes 20, 25, and 27, above.

46. See Reichard, *Navaho Religion,* p. 90.

47. Hill, *Navaho Humor,* p. 23.

48. Ibid., p. 21.

49. Hennigh, "Control of Incest," p. 368.

50. On order and Navajo ritual, see Reichard, *Navaho Religion,* pp. 183, 80-81; in the remainder of this discussion it is important to keep in mind that culturally the Navajos are "nomadic," that their whole view of life seems based on a sense of where they stand in relation to a changing landscape. As Hoijer has pointed out, this characteristic is reflected deeply by the Navajo language, which defines position by withdrawal of motion, which has very few nouns, and which most often uses substantives which are actually descriptions of movements: *haniibǫǫz,* lit., "a hoop-like object has rolled out," means "full moon." See Harry Hoijer, "Cultural Implications of Some Navaho Linguistic Categories," in *Language in Culture and Society,* ed. Dell Hymes (New York: Harper & Row, 1964), pp. 142-48.

51. Reichard, *Navaho Religion,* p. 5.

52. Hill, *Navaho Humor,* p. 23.

53. Reichard, *Navaho Religion,* p. 119.

54. Reichard, *Navaho Religion,* pp. 422-26.

55. Hymes, "Discovering Oral Performance," pp. 453-54.

56. We are much indebted to Dell Hymes for helping to clarify this matter in personal correspondence. Besides having dedicated a large part of his life to translating and understanding Native American literature, he has unselfishly encouraged and urged on many of those now seriously engaged in this field. His personal and scholarly generosity are in large part responsible for the current standing of this profession.

57. To move from this level of discourse to a deeper awareness of how

these stories fit into Navajo culture and world view, one must at least consult Gary Witherspoon's tour de force, *Language and Art in the Navajo Universe* (Ann Arbor: University of Michigan Press, 1977); it treats such subjects as creativity through language, order and harmony, and such matters as brought up in this article by showing how they grow out of and relate to Navajo language. Among other things, Witherspoon notes that there are only a few conjugations of the verb "to be," but 356,200 distinct conjugations for the verb "to go," giving a statistical support to the well-known concept put forward by nearly every specialist on the Navajos that the Navajo world view is far more interested in movement than in physical stasis. This work should now be obligatory for anyone wishing to see Navajo culture more fully.

DELL H. HYMES

Reading Clackamas Texts

I want to show that close attention to a detail of language can illuminate the meaning that Native American myths must have had for their narrators and can have for us today.

An odd beginning, you may say. Do we not know that literature exists in the medium of words? Do we not live amidst a smorgasbord of efforts to deal with verbal form? Not, sad to say, in the study of Native American narratives. The reviver of serious attention among scholars to the riches of Native American collections, discoverer of the principle of transformational inversion in the creation of myths, Lévi-Strauss, has set aside the control of linguistic detail as both impractical for the work he intended and of little importance to structure. The man who made possible my work here, by seeking out and preserving the texts on which it is based, Melville Jacobs, disparaged focus on the linguistics as a route to meaning and style. This is not the place to speculate on the reasons for such views, but I believe that a basic element is that those who take an interest in Native American materials do not find in place an adequate philology on which to build, and lack the patience or at least the opportunity to bring such philology about. Again and again, we are reduced to dealing with literature in translation, unable to control what lies behind the translation.

The problems of understanding what Native American narrators have intended and expressed is difficult enough. It is far more difficult if, in a certain sense, we do not know what they said.

117

Such a circumstance would not be tolerated in serious study of classical Greek and Latin literature, of the Bible, of Old English poetry, of the Russian novel, and the like. It should not be tolerated in serious study of Native American literature. A tacit double standard, and the shameful neglect of institutional support for scholarship in the subject, permit it to continue.

Even if one agrees in principle with the position just stated, it is not easy to point to an example of the difference that adequate philology would make. It is hard to point to an example of a *reading* of a Native American text in the Native American language which is dependent for its interpretation on features of the language itself. I hope that this paper will provide an example of the kind required. So far as I know, it is the first instance of developing an interpretation of the meaning of texts based on the use of a device that cannot be represented in English translation.[1]

The device—I did not know it to be one to begin with—consists of variations in the prefix to noun stems in Clackamas Chinook. The texts were recorded by Melville Jacobs from Victoria Howard in 1929 and 1930, shortly before she died. They are all we have of Clackamas, beyond another short paragraph once jotted down by Boas, and the richest of what we have for any of the Chinookan language groups, indeed for almost any of the Native American peoples of the Pacific Northwest states. That richness makes them a fulcrum for the interpretation of what is preserved of neighboring literatures, as I try to show in a book-length study from which the present piece is derived.

A word on the language and the device. Before white people arrived, rather closely related languages were spoken along most of the Columbia from its mouth at the Pacific Ocean to a point near the present site of the Dalles Dam some two hundred miles inland. The people on the Washington and Oregon sides of the mouth of the river are known to us as the Shoalwater and Clatsop, respectively. A little in from the mouth were the Kathlamet, reaching westward fairly close to Portland. Just south of Portland near present Oregon City, were the Clackamas, harvesting salmon at the falls near Oregon City and hunting and gathering in the hinterland. To their east along the Columbia were the Cascades and Hood River groups, and farthest east, the Wasco on the Oregon side and the Wishram on the Washington side. Just a few speakers of Wasco-Wishram (there is no linguistic difference) survive today.

In all the Chinookan languages a noun is not a complete word unless its stem is preceded by a prefix. There are exceptions to this, in that speakers are able to cite the stem of the word—especially, it seems, the name of a creature—if they wish. The speech of the youngest generation to learn something of the language has sometimes been criticized by older speakers for dropping these prefixes, and it indeed seems that the prefixes are the last layer of structure to be fixed in the noun. The contemporary situation may be influenced by the rise in the nineteenth century of Chinook Jargon, a trade language based in important part on Chinookan vocabulary, but dropping Chinookan grammatical machinery, as is normally the case with pidgin lingua francas. In the middle and late nineteenth century surviving Chinookan speakers usually knew this prefixless code, alongside their other languages.

The prefixes have jointly a lexical and a grammatical role. On the one hand, change of prefix can change the meaning of a word. All the prefixes of concern to us can be characterized as expressing third-person meanings (and are clearly derived from third-person pronoun elements), distinguishing between singular, dual, and plural in number, and between "masculine," "feminine," and "neuter" in the singular itself. Lexical gender matches biological gender with words for human beings and creatures of a certain size: *a-duiha* is "cow," *i-duiha* is "steer"; *a-k'ask'as* is "girl," *i-k'ask'as* is "boy." Some nouns are inherently dual, never occurring with a singular prefix (for example, the words for "eyes," "testicles," "double-barreled shotgun"). There are a variety of interesting specifics of this sort, more than need to be considered for our purpose.

The point about the prefixes on which this study focuses is that they do not differ as to number or gender. At first glance, the difference appears arbitrary. *a-* is third-person singular feminine, and so is *wa-*. *i-* is third-person singular masculine, and so is *wi-*.

The great linguist Edward Sapir once suggested that the occurrence of *wa-* or *a-*, *wi-* or *i-*, depended on the length of the following noun stem. The forms with *w-* occurred with monosyllabic stems, preserved or elaborated to balance their brevity. One might also suspect that the variation reflects a change in progress in the language, a change not yet brought to completion. That idea would fit better the fact that one and the same noun stem can sometimes be found with both alternatives, as is the case with the names of interest here. One might suspect dialect difference or dialect mixture in the materials collected by Jacobs, since Victoria Howard reported hearing some of her narratives from her mother's mother and some from her mother-in-law, who came from a somewhat more easterly community along the Columbia. For reasons tedious to expound here, none of these explanations holds. A reading of the texts points to the use of *wa-* or *a-* as motivated by expressive intent, by point of view. Recognition of this device deepens understanding of the texts.

Specifically, a reading of the texts shows that the significance of the naming of Grizzly Women depends upon the placement as well as the shape of a prefix.

Placement has to do with where the Grizzly Woman is named, whether in the title or in the text, and at what point in the text.

Prefix has to do with two levels of choice. One is the choice of a singular or nonsingular prefix from the regular paradigmatic set of noun-initial prefixes. The dual and plural prefixes seem to go together with a view of Grizzly Woman as a *type* encountered in adventures although some such Grizzly Women are indeed named with a singular prefix. The second level of choice is of *wa-*, *a-*, or zero. It is this choice that appears to be most frequent, subtle, and revealing of point of view. In this essay I am especially concerned with the importance of the distinctions between *wa-* and *a-*.

Within the texts in which the singular prefix varies, a hitherto unsuspected consistency begins to emerge under analytic scrutiny. The consistency has to do with the point at which the Grizzly Woman is named, placement reflecting point of view. In the original of "Grizzly Woman Pursued Him" (text 134, see note 1), the title has *wa-*, while the text names the Ogress once with *a-* (p. 558, l. 7). She is so named at the peripety of the action. Old Watcheeno's father has fled from her to a tree, and shot at her vainly while she has been digging up the tree. Out of arrows, he thinks of starting a fire. When he throws down burning dry limbs and moss, Grizzly Woman sees them, throws herself on the bundle, and puts it out. It is at this point that the action of the story reverses direction. It changes from her pursuit and digging to her being diverted and drawn away by fire. To name her at this turning point seems to heighten the confrontation, identifying just whom the man is escaping and besting. That the naming is with *a-*, not *wa-*, suggests that Grizzly Woman occurs here in the role of a dangerous creature of the forest, not in any role of kinship and personal identity. Indeed, there is nothing of the latter in the adventure.

Three texts alternate *wa-* and *a-* (texts 9, 16, 34). In "Coyote Went around the Land" (text 9), Coyote meets women who are gathering grass. They tell him that Grizzly Woman covers them with it, then bakes them (as food for her husband). Here (p. 97, l. 5) she is named with *wa-*. Coyote succeeds in pushing Grizzly Woman into the fire (rather like Gretel saving Hansel), where she will be left for her returning husband to eat unawares. The grateful women take Coyote to their houses, telling people, "This man saved our hearts; we have killed Grizzly Woman." Here (p. 98, l. 11), she is named with *a-*.

On the assumption that the difference is significant, not accidental, the contrast in connotation is clear. With *wa-*, Grizzly Woman is a living, controlling, threatening being. With *a-*, she is dead.

In "Black Bear and Grizzly Woman and Their Sons" (text 16), both women are named a number of times. Black Bear herself is named always with *a-* (*skintwa*). Her name occurs once with *wa-* in reference to her children (p. 146, l. 12), signaling a shift in generation (from Black Bear herself to her children) and a reversal in power (from Grizzly Woman's family to Black Bear's). Grizzly has returned from finally killing Black Bear while out berrying. The three-line sequence goes: she went, she went homeward, she arrived. It is followed by a sequence which begins: "Black Bear's children were going about by the river. / They did not see their mother. / Now he (her eldest son, the hero of the rest of the story with a name-title of his own, Wasgukmayli) thought, / 'Now she has killed her.' He said nothing to her." From now on the action centers on the revenge and escape effected by Black Bear's children under the leadership of Wasgukmayli. The placement seems at a turning point, as in the case of the naming in "Grizzly Woman Pursued Him."

The Ogress herself is consistently named with *wa-* in the

first part of the myth. The contrast to the *a-* with which Black Bear is named is consistent with the difference between the two in power and control. *Wa-* is retained for Grizzly Woman's name in reference to her children at the point of their being killed by Black Bear's son (p. 147, l. 8), after she has gone off again. Perhaps this heightens the identification; it would seem to retain the threat of her own revenge in full force. A change to *a-* with her name comes when Wasgukmayli halloos to Crane to take him and the rest of Black Bear's children across the river because Grizzly Woman (here *a-*) is following them (p. 150, l. 16). By now the story has shown her deceived as to the stew she eats on her return (it has her child in it); deceived by the dog left behind as to the direction in which Black Bear's children have escaped; deceived by a trick in which excrement falls on her from a tree. She has indeed "died" (become unconscious) as a result of the last deception, and is in that state, so far as the text goes, at the time she is named in the halloo to Crane.

The Ogress is *wa-* again as she revives and takes up the pursuit (p. 151, l. 5). She is not named again until the end—not in her drowning, after Crane tips her into the river, or when her vagina is picked at by Crows, or when she smears its blood on her face, or when she journeys through the woods to ask each tree its opinion of her looks, rewarding those who flatter her by endowing them as useful to the people who will come. At long last she reaches a house where people are saying: "When Wasgukmayli and his younger brothers went, it was really long long ago." Then, the text says, Grizzly Woman (*wa-*) ate them up. She repeats as if in a dazed stupor what the people had said, and that Grizzly Woman (*wa-*) ate them up (p. 156, ll. 3, 5). In sum, she has *wa-* when she is in control, pursuing, eating people, but *a-* once when temporarily she is "dead."

It may be significant that Grizzly Woman is not named in the long epilogue to the main story. It is in the main story, widely known in native North America, that she is the Grizzly Ogress who kills kin and pursues people; and it is when the main story is recalled in the coda, and she eats people, that her name (with *wa-*) returns. In the interval—an interval not unique to the Clackamas, but shared with the Kathlamet version of the story—Grizzly Woman is variously a victim, crazed or absurd, and caught up in a long sequence of looking ahead to what the world should be like when the Indian people come. When she interrogates trees, and rewards or punishes them for their answers by making them useful or useless to the people who will come, she is enacting the fundamental premise of the Indian world view that Robert Redfield called "participant maintenance." People and nature are joined in a relationship of mutual benevolence, and it is a punishment to trees to be excluded. The same role with trees is taken by Skunk in a long story I had the privilege of hearing once from Mrs. Blanche Tohet, a Sahaptin speaker. There the role balances Skunk's part otherwise as comic victim, while here in the Clackamas story it balances Grizzly Woman's part as monstrous aggressor. Perhaps we have here an indication that dramatic balance could be a factor in the transformation of myths, the ordaining of the usefulness of trees being thought suitable for such balance.

In "Gitskux and His Older Brother" (text 34), the name of the Grizzly Ogress begins with the prefix *a-* four, perhaps five, times. Each fits easily into the semantic distinction that has emerged. When Gitskux and his older brother are out hunting, their bows break; they return to find Grizzly Woman simply there in their home: *uXt Akitsimani* "(she) is there Akitsimani" (p. 316, l. 10). In the next scene, the two brothers have brought back a little raccoon, which Grizzly Woman takes as a pet although the elder brother's two children cry for it. While Grizzly Woman is absent, the elder brother's first wife kills the coon. Grizzly Woman is named as absent with *a-* (p. 317, l. 7). She becomes angry because her husband's younger brother has brought back a raccoon for the children, while she has none; and, left alone, she kills the raccoon. She and the first wife fight; she kills the other wife and dons her skin. The wife had foreseen this and warned the children, and Grizzly Woman in disguise makes certain mistakes. Gitskux feeds her heavily, as his elder brother's late wife had advised, and she torpidly falls asleep. He is then able to take off her sister-in-law's skin: "Oh dear! Akitsimani is the one lying here!" (p. 319, l. 15).

This section of the story ends with Grizzly Woman being killed, but not successfully, since her bones were not mashed up and blown away. Eventually she returns, kills the wife and people, and takes Gitskux captive away with her. The elder brother has another, good wife come to him, and then two sons, who become big. At that point the new wife inquires and is told that her husband had not come there alone, but had had a younger brother: "Grizzly Woman took him, maybe she ate him" (p. 324, 1. 11). The Ogress is named without prefix, *kitsimani,* but I suspect that the form is *a-kitsimani.* The preceding word, *gagigitga,* "she took him," ends with /-a/, and it is a regular rule of Wasco that /a + a/ will coalesce into a single vowel, if not separated by a pause. Since *gagitga kitsimani* is a single phrase, it is likely that the /a/ that is printed at the end of the first word stands as well for an /a/ that begins the second. The point in the story is analogous to that in the story of Grizzly Bear and Black Bear at which Black Bear's escaping children halloo to Crane. In the latter story, Grizzly Bear was temporarily "dead." In this story, she is indeed remote. Attention has turned to the elder brother and the steps by which he is united with his new, supernaturally powerful wife; as said, two boys have been born to them and have become big. Throughout this long section (p. 322, 1. 2 to p. 326, 1. 10), Grizzly Woman has not been mentioned, even by a pronominal prefix. She has been offstage in a state of silent "hold."

The elder brother and his new wife rescue the younger brother, Gitskux, and kill Grizzly Woman, but again fail to kill her completely. She again returns, kills and skins the wife, and dons the skin as a disguise; she makes some mistakes in accustomed conduct, falls asleep, and is killed, this time for good, and the new wife restored. At the point at which Gitskux is removing the wife's skin from Grizzly Woman, she is named: "Grizzly Woman (*a-*) sleeps" (p. 330, 1. 13). Nothing could be more appropriate than to underline her passivity by a prefix here, as the rhetorical lengthening in the verb also shows (*u:::::qiw*), as may also the "historical present" tense.

The questions with "Gitskux and His Older Brother" arise with the use of *wa-.* Most of the occurrences of *wa-,* to be sure, fit the sense of purposive activity that other texts have shown. The Grizzly Ogress is named when she comes to the two brothers (p. 316, 1. 5), when she goes and lies down with the elder brother as his unasked-for second wife (p. 316, 1. 11), when she claims the little raccoon for herself (p. 317, 1. 2), and when she plays with it while her husband's two children cry (p. 317, 1. 4). Again, she is named when anger acts on her about the second raccoon (p. 317, 1. 12), when she takes Gitskux away after she has killed the elder brother's wife (p. 321, l. 18), and when Gitskux's bow breaks and he knows from the sign that "Grizzly Woman has come now" (p. 329, l. 15). At that point in the story, she is not dead or remote. She has just returned for the last time, killed the elder brother's wife, skinned her, put on her skin, dragged her to the rear of the house, laid her down, and covered her. (This rapid sequence of six actions is in lines 7–9 of page 329).

Two occurrences of *wa-* with the naming of the Grizzly Ogress do *not* seem to fit. The immediately related verb is itself a verb, not of action, but of the passive state. Thus, a little after she has gotten angry about the second little raccoon, it is said, "Grizzly Woman was alone there" (p. 317, l. 16). The verb is the same as in saying earlier that she is there, namely, *uXt*. The only difference in sentence context is an initial pronoun, *ayma*, "she only." But this pronoun is an indication of a difference that depends on the rhetorical-poetic form of the scene as a whole.

Here is the scene. Notice that the Grizzly Woman is named in it three times. (Such patterning of the naming of an important element in a scene is common in Chinookan.) At the outset of the scene she is named for the first time, when she first comes to the family, with *wa-* (*wakitsimani*). At the end of the scene she is named with *wa-* when she intrudes herself into the elder brother's marriage bed. In the middle of the scene she is named as an object of perception—what the two brothers see when they hurry home and enter. This naming is with *a-* (*Akitsimani*). It occurs at the end of a three-line verse, and indeed of a three-verse stanza; final position in a sequence is usual for the naming of an object of perception in texts in all the Chinookan dialects.[2]

The next incident is that of the little raccoon that the hunters bring back and Grizzly Woman claims, despite the cries of the two children. The first wife is upset at their crying and kills the raccoon when Grizzly Woman is absent. When the hunters bring a second raccoon, Gitskux gives it to the children, who play with it all day long while Grizzly Woman, on the other hand, gets angry. Now comes the stanza containing *Wa*kitsimani with the verb *uXt*, "(she) is there." The organization of the whole shows that she is not there as an object of perception on the part of others, but as one left alone with an opportunity for action. The initial "only" of the first verse is pregnant with that opportunity.

Now they lived there,
 all day long the boys played with it;
on a certain day they went to the water,
 they went for a swim;
Only she, Grizzly Woman, is there.

Now she for her part cleaned up
 she clubbed the raccoon,
  she killed it.

The two children got back,
 right away they went to where their raccoon was;
they saw it is dead,
 they wept;
now the two women quarreled.

Soon now they jumped up at each other,
 they fought each other;
she killed her,
 she skinned her;
she put it on herself:
 the children fled.

She called out to them,
 she would tell them:
  "Come! Come!
  Soon your uncle (and father) will come back."
But no,
 they would not go inside.

The second apparent exception to the rule that has emerged for the alternation of *wa-* and *a-* also yields to a close reading in the context of the discourse structure, as well as to the literal translation. The sentence in question is translated reasonably enough in the collection as, "She sat on Grizzly Woman who was underneath." The context is the return of Grizzly Woman from the first attempt to kill her, and the immediate outbreak of a fight between the two wives. The English translation would imply that Grizzly Woman is in a passive state. The Clackamas wording offers a different impression. First, it begins with the word "underneath," as if to convey something contrary to expectation, which, coming at the outset of a verse, may be changed. Second, the verb does not refer to the first wife, or to any specific person, as the agent sitting on Grizzly Woman. The place of the transitive actor is occupied by the impersonal prefix *q-*; agency is displaced by a construction which focuses on the formal object, Wakitsimani. Third, this is the first naming of the Grizzly Woman on her return. The naming is in a line which begins the second verse of the stanza, the verse which develops the action from the situation set in the first verse to the point of the action of the third. And of course Wakitsimani may be down, but not inactive; she is in the midst of a fight.

Here is a revised translation of the entire scene (320:5–12):

(A) I do not know how long,
   now again it got back to them.
  The two fought,
   they were fighting,
    the two children were crying and screaming.
  People said,
   "Dear oh dear! Our chief's wives are fighting."
    They gathered on account of the two fighting.

(B) Wakitsimani was sat on under*neath*.
   Soon she got herself up,
    now again she threw her down.
     The people would call out (excitedly),
      Wakitsimani got angry now.

(C) She thought,
   "Now she made me ill."
  Now she became a dangerous being,
   she swallowed her.
  Now she ate up *all* the people.
  (My mother's mother used to say,
   "only she would eat people.
   The rest of the Grizzly Women did not eat people.
   They only killed them.")

(D) She recalled her sister-in-law,
   she thought,
    "I didn't swallow her."
  She vomited:
   "Oh *no*."
    She did not swallow her (again).
  She went to the river,
   she is at the water,
    she washes her head.

(E)   She leapt on her,
           she seized her,
               she broke off her head.
       It went into the water,
           it floated away.
       In vain she tried repeatedly to seize it,
           it floated away.

The third verse (C) is pivotal, constituting an outcome for the series of the first three verses, and an onset for the series of the last three within the stanza of five. We can observe this pivotal role of the middle verse in other stanzas; it seems to express a principle that can be involved at all levels of organization, from five-line verse to five-act narrative.

Prefix choice and rhetorical-poetic form: the alternation of wa-/a. In sum, the choice of *wa-* or *a-* is not random, nor is it to be explained within the immediate sentence. The choice involves an active or passive state of the named actor; but the active or passive, transitive or intransitive, causative or stative character of the accompanying verb construction or verb stem is not a criterion in itself. The state of the named actor depends upon the use of the sentence in the action of the story, an action that is shaped and expressed through the rhetorical-poetic organization of the discourse. That organization employs modes of ordering experience recurrent in Chinookan narrative, and, indeed, in conversation to this day: the threefold sequence with its logic of onset, ongoing, outcome; the placement of something perceived or something said as a local outcome; the framing of action through an introduction, first, of key actors, and then of a morally emblematic activity characteristic of one or more of them; and recurrent use of local parallelism, and of change in "scene/agent ratio" (to use Kenneth Burke's term), such changes in place, time, or leading actor often being accompanied by particles such as "now," "soon," "a little later" in Clackamas.

In the Clackamas texts that enter into this essay, as in Chinookan texts generally, there is constant recurrence of formal means, together with individuality of the overall shape. No single formal criterion serves to identify rhetorical-poetical form, nor does any set of criteria. One comes to learn to expect the principles stated in the preceding paragraph not to be violated. It comes to be easy to block out the rhetorical-poetic form of a passage. Yet blocking out is not the same as the final version. The parallelisms, repetitions, contours specific to a passage have to become vivid to the mind. One has to reconstitute a version of narrative intention, of intended narrative effect. To do so is not to be arbitrary. One is forced to enter more deeply into a presumably intended narrative effect by the loose ends that blocking out may leave. Entering more deeply means giving attention to the place of a passage in the overall narrative design, and becoming sensitive to the formal options which make formal sense of the passage in hand. Sometimes, most notably, action moves threefold with three verbs, clippety, clippety, clop; sometimes it moves pairwise with two verbs, this this, that that, thus thus. One may have blocked out this this, that that, thus thus, but be forced to reconsider by failure of fit. Confidence comes from the experience of fit being there to find, and of coming to experience pattern without conscious analysis.

Inquiry into a minor, almost neglectable, variation in grammar has turned out to implicate the major modes of the organization of discourse. In a larger context the choice of the shape of a prefix with apparently constant meaning, feminine singular, has turned out to imply an additional dimension of meaning. *Wa-* has to do with an active, *a-* with a passive state, in those texts in which the two alternate. In those texts, the shape of prefix varies with the point of view.

This finding opens up a need for investigation of the use of both *wa-* and *wi-* throughout the Clackamas texts and other Chinookan materials. It poses a question for the history of the language as well: Is there a source within Chinookan, perhaps within Penutian, for such an element? A $^{*}w$- "active"? Could the Takelma prefix *wa-*, of demonstrative pronoun origin, but used in an instrumental meaning before noun stems, be distantly connected? Or has the active/passive contrast in the discourse use of *w-* emerged within recent times in Chinookan itself? The association of "active" with *w-* could reflect an old, otherwise submerged, state of affairs, or the recent dynamics of narration, the existence of a variation attracting intentional use.

Whichever be the case, there remain two Clackamas texts in

which there is a variation of prefix, but without *wa-*. The first of these especially shows understanding to depend on the overall shaping of the narrative. After examining the alternations in themselves, we can venture a more general view of the role of *wa-* and all prefixes in such alternations.

Variable Prefix and Point of View: a-/∅-

In "Grizzly Woman Began to Kill People" (text 17) the Grizzly Woman is identified with *wa-* only in the title of the myth: *"Wakitsimani gaqdudinanmCk idElxam."* Within the text, the alternation is between *a-* and *∅-*. The norm of the text is *∅-*. Out of thirteen namings of the Grizzly Woman, eleven are with *∅-*, only two with *a-*. This matter of proportion must be taken up, but let us first attend to the contexts of the text in question, a translation of which follows.[3] Subsequent references will be given *both* to my translation by parts ("act" with majuscule Roman numerals, "scene" with miniscule Roman numerals, and "stanza" with majuscule letters) and to page and line in Jacobs's original publication of the text.

Grizzly Woman Began to Kill People

PART ONE. Grizzly Woman Deceives and Kills Women.

Preface.

Act   I.   Grizzly Woman becomes a headman's wife.
       II.   Grizzly Woman takes women for camas (1).
     III.   Grizzly Woman takes women for camas (2).
     IV.   Grizzly Woman takes women for camas (3).
      V.   Grizzly Woman takes women for camas (4).

PART TWO. Waterbug Overcomes Grizzly Woman

Act VI.   Grizzly Woman discovered.
    VII.   Grizzly Woman disclosed.
   VIII.   Grizzly Woman overcome.
     IX.   Grizzly Woman escaped.
      X.   Grizzly Woman destroyed.

130

ONE. Grizzly Woman Deceives and Kills Women.

Preface   They lived on and on in their village;
             their headman's house was in the center.

I.   [Grizzly Woman becomes a headman's wife]
A   Soon now,
     a woman reached him;
        they said,
          "Some woman has reached our headman";
            now they lived on there.

B   In spring,
     she went I don't know where,
        she came back at evening:
           Oh dear! she brought back camas;
            now she began to share it about.

C   They told her,
      "Where did you gather them?"
    She told them,
       "Well, I reached a burned-over place,
         It's just camas there,
           The camas stand thick."

D   They told her,
      "Goodness, whenever you go again,
         We'll follow you."
    "Very well,"
      she told them,
        "Perhaps tomorrow."

E   "Indeed. We will follow you too."
    "All right,"
      she told them.

II.   [Grizzly Woman takes women for camas (1).]
A   In the morning,
     now they go,
        I don't know how many canoes went,
         they arrived,
           they went ashore,
             they dug.

B   It became evening,
     now they camped;
        they said,
          "Later tomorrow, then . . ."
          They lay down to sleep the night.

C   At daybreak,
      she took her arrow-spear,
        she went among them,
          she pierced their hearts,
            she killed them *all*.

D   Now it was day,
      now she carried them off;
        she laid them down,
        she hid their paddles;
        she thought,
          "Now I will go,
          I will go home."

E   She brought those very camas, the people's;
   She arrived at the village,
      she told them,
        "They sent these to you."
   She went to another house,
      she told them,
        "Later tomorrow,
          Then I will go fetch them."
   They told her,
      "We will follow you too."
   "To be sure,"
      she told them.

III. [Grizzly Woman takes women for camas (2)]
A   In the morning,
      now they get ready,
   Now they go, three canoes;
      they went,
        they arrived;
   Their (predecessors') canoes are tied,
      they tied their canoes too,
        they went ashore.
   She told them,
      "Oh *dear,* perhaps they are over yonder.
      There there are even lots more camas.
      Stay here first.
      Later tomorrow,
        Then we'll go in that direction."
   "Indeed,"
      they told her;
        they dug.

B   It became evening,
>they (the camas) were brought up,
>>they started fires.

Soon,
>now Grizzly Woman arrived on the run,
>>she told them,
>>>"Oh dear . . . , now they have lots of camas;
>>>They tell me,
>>>>'Perhaps we will cook them right here.'"

"Indeed,"
>they told her.

C   Now they began to eat,
>they ceased:
>>*no* Grizzly Woman.

Soon they heard singing;
>they said,
>>"Oh dear! they are singing!
>>>Listen to them!"
>>>>They listened.

Soon she arrived on the run,
>she told them,
>>"Why are you silent?
>>Yonder those folks are singing."

"To be sure!"
>they told her,
>>"We hear them";
>>>they said,
>>>>"Let us sing too."

Now they began to sing.
>They ceased.
>>They lay down to sleep.

D   At daybreak,
>now again she went among them,
>>she numbed them (with her spirit-power).

Now again she took her arrow-spear,
>she pierced their hearts,
>>she killed them all.

In the morning,
>now again she carried them off,
>>she laid them all
>>>where she had put away the first ones.

E   She gathered up their camas,
>she put it in (her bag);

Now she went home,
    she arrived;
Now again she informed them the same way:
    "They won't come (today),
        After a while,
            Then they will come,"
                she told them.
"Indeed,"
    they told her.
Now others said,
    "We will go too."

IV. [Grizzly Woman takes women for camas (3)]

i   A   In the morning,
    now they got ready,
        they went;
            again she took them,
                they arrived,
                    they went ashore.

    B   They became somehow (disturbed).
She told them,
    "Right here they kept working.
    Perhaps they moved off a little yonder,
        There are even lots more camas."
"Indeed,"
    they told her;
        they dug.

    C   One said,
    "What do you think?
    Seems a long long time since these (were) digging places."
"Surely,"
    they told her,
        "We noticed (that about) them."
They ceased.

ii A   In the evening,
    they camped there;
        they said,
            "It's not as it should be,
                Something somehow (is wrong)."

    B   Soon,
    now Grizzly arrived on the run,
        she told them,
            "Why are you so silent?

Those yonder,
　　they are singing,
　　　they are giggling,
　　　　they are laughing—
　　　　　those who came first—
　　Now they have baked their camas there."
"Ind*ee*d,"
　　they told her,
　　　"It's just (that) we became somehow (disturbed)."
"G*oo*dness!"
　　she told them,
　　　"What for?
　　　Soon,
　　　　again they will begin dancing.
　　　Suppose I run,
　　　　I go to see them again."
　　　　　She ran.

C　Soon,
　　　as they stayed there,
　　　　they heard singing.
　　They said,
　　　"Truly it is so;
　　　Now they sing,
　　　Listen."
　　"Surely,"
　　　they said;
　　　　they stayed there.

iii　Now again she got back to them,
　　　she told them,
　　　　"You start to sing too!"
　　"To be sure,"
　　　they told her;
　　　　they started to sing in vain,
　　　　　no,
　　　　　　they ceased.
　　They lay down to sleep;
　　　Grizzly also lay down;
　　　　they slept.

iv　Now Grizzly Woman arose,
　　　she numbed them (with her spirit-power),
　　　　she got her arrow-spear.
　　Now again she went among them,
　　　she pierced their hearts,
　　　　she killed them all.

       In the morning,
          now again she carried them
             where she had put down those first ones;
               all done;
                  she ceased.

v   A   Now she put their camas in (her bag);
       Now she went back,
          she arrived;
       Now again she told them the same way,
          "They sent these to you."

      B   "Indeed,"
          they told her;
       "The first ones who went,
          now they are baking them."

      C   "Oh dear! Let us go tomorrow too!"
       "Yes,"
          she told them.

      V.   [Grizzly Woman takes women for camas (4)]
i   A   In the morning,
          now they get ready,
             they go;
          they arrived,
             they went ashore;
          they arrived
             where their (predecessors') fire was.

      B   One burst out crying.
       She was told,
          "Why are you making a bad omen for yourself?"
       She told them,
          "No.
          Somehow something (is wrong).
          It happens to our people
             where you are looking."
       "No::::::!
       A long long time (since) their fire,
          now it is gone there,"
             they told her.
       "Never mind! She keeps saying nothing at all!" (said Grizzly).

      C   They went to dig,
          they dug;
             that one tries in vain,
               she will become silent,
                  now again she will cry.

ii   A   They ceased at evening,
           they went to their camp,
              they sat;
                they said,
                  "We will not build a fire."

      B   Soon,
           now again Grizzly arrived on the run,
              she told them,
                "Why have you become this (way)?"
           They told her,
              "This one has become ill."
           "Indeed. Soon she will cease (to be)."

      C   Now again they lay down to sleep.
           She arrived on the run,
              she told them,
                "Oh *dear*! Have you lay down to sleep there?"
           They told her,
              "Yes . . . Later tomorrow morning,
                we will dig."
           "Indeed,"
              she told them,
                "I will go inform them."
           They pay no attention to her.
           She ran.
           Soon,
              they heard:
                "Oh *dear*! they are singing."
           They said,
              "Listen! they are singing."
           One said,
              she said,
                "Do you really think it is true?"
           They became silent.

iii   Now again she hurried to them,
              she told them,
                "They were going to come;
                I told them,
                  '*Long* ago they lay down to sleep.
                  Nevermind.'
                Now I will lie down too."
           Now she lay down.
           They slept.

iv   Now again she numbed them (with her spirit-power).

Now she arose,

    she got her arrow-spear;

Now again she went among them,

    she pierced their hearts.

In the morning,

    now again she carried them.

All done . . .

    she ceased.

v   A   She put their camas in (her bag),

    a very few.

Now she went back,

    she arrived,

      she shared their camas around.

   B   She told them,

    "They became lazy,

      They dug a few,

        They said,

          'Later tomorrow morning, then.'"

"Indeed,"

    they told her.

   C   Now some again said,

    "We too will go in the morning."

Her sister-in-law also said,

    "I also will go in the morning."

Right away her little younger sister said,

    "I also will go, older sister!"

   D   She (Grizzly) said,

    "Already you also!

    Why should you go along?"

She (Waterbug) said,

    "I will just go along with my older sister."

   E   "*No!*",

    she told her,

      "You will not go."

She said,

    "I will go!"

She told her,

    "No."

"I will go."

Her older sister told her (Grizzly),

    "She is just saying that to you.

      We two (you and I) will go in the morning.

TWO. Waterbug Overcomes Grizzly Woman.

VI. [Grizzly Woman discovered]
A In the morning,
    now they got ready,
        the very first is Water Bug;
            she went,
                she hid in the canoe.
    They went to the river,
        they got in their canoe,
            they went.
    Grizzly turned and looked,
        she saw her,
            she said,
                "Dear oh dear! I told you not to come."
    She pays *no* attention to her there.
    They went,
        they arrived,
            they went ashore.
B Grizzly Woman forgot (about her);
    she forgot,
        she did not take her older sister's paddles.
    Water Bug took them,
        she went,
            she hid them;
    She ran about,
        she got *all* those paddles (previously hidden by Grizzly),
        she moved them away.
C Now she went ashore,
    she reached her older sister,
        she told her,
            "Those here are *all* dead.
                Let us go."
    Now the two went,
        they reached them,
            Dear oh dear . . . there are corpses.
    The two sat,
        they wept;
            she told her older sister,
                "Wash your face;
                    She will become suspicious."

VII. [Grizzly Woman disclosed]
A   The two arrived,
      they informed them;
        they wept;
          they ceased,
            they washed their faces.
  Water Bug told them,
    "Say nothing at all.
    When she will tell us,
      'You should sing,'
        You should do that.
          Be very careful!"
  Soon,
    now she hurried to them;
  she nudged her older sister,
    she nudged her;
  she said,
    "Now she will tell us!"
B   She told them,
    "Why are you so *still*?
    You are lying to the people about something, Water Bug!"
  She pays *no* attention to her.
  She told them,
    "Oh *dear*! Now they are drying their cooked camas."
  She nudged her older sister.
  She (Grizzly) ceased,
    now she left them.
C   Again now the two informed them, Water Bug (and her sister).
    She said,
      "Be careful!"
  "Yes indeed,"
    they told her.
  "You are not to be first,
    Her plan is to kill me first";
      she informed them of everything,
      she told them,
        "When she falls asleep,
        Now we will leave here."
  "Indeed,"
    they told her.
  She ran to the river,
    she picked up shells,
      she brought them to her older sister.

VIII. [Grizzly Woman foiled]

i   Now it *became* night,

        they had lain down to sleep;

          she got to them.

      "Surely,"

        she said,

          "Now you lied about something to them."

      She paid no attention,

        she said nothing whatever;

          they had lain down to sleep.

ii A   Grizzly Woman said,

        "Now I too,

        Now I lie down."

      Water Bug picked up a lot of wood.

    B   She (Grizzly) told her,

        "Why will you make a fire all night?

          So that is why you came—(to be a nuisance)—

        You're thinking,

          Maybe some young man will get to your sister!"

      She paid no attention.

    C   "Sleep acts on them,

        In the morning they will get up,

          They will dig."

      She paid no attention,

        she lay down to sleep,

          she put those shells on her eyes.

iii A   Soon,

        the fire went down a little;

          Grizzly Woman arose slowly, silently.

      She saw her,

        she nudged her older sister,

          the two see her.

      She went up to them,

        she looked at Water Bug:

          she is watching her.

    B   "Oh, goodness!"

        she told her,

          "Aren't you going to go to sleep?

            Youths are going about."

      "Oooo,"

        she went,

          Water Bug went (feigning sudden fright at being awakened).

141

C   She got up,
        she fixed the fire,
            she put large pieces of wood on the fire.
   "Ahh,"
        she told her,
            "Why indeed are you going to make a fire all night?"
   She told her nothing whatever,
        she lay down again.

iv A   Soon,
        the fire went down.
   Now again Grizzly Woman got up,
        she approached slowly, silently;
   She (Water Bug) heard,
        "T'áLmu t'áLmu."

B   "Ooooo!"
        went Water Bug
   "Oh *dear*! Aren't you going to go to sleep?"
   "Oooo I was dreaming,
        I saw a bloody arrow-spear."
   "Goodness! Now she will lie to them;
        Leave them alone,
            They are sleeping."
   Now again she lay down to sleep.

C   Water Bug got up,
        again she put more wood on the fire.
   She told her,
        "So that is why you came!
            You might wake people all night."
   Waterbug lay down to sleep.

v   Now it was close to dawn,
        now Grizzly Woman became sleepy,
            she would nod off to sleep.
   She would wake up,
        she would get up slowly, silently,
            she would look at Water Bug:
               she is watching her;
                   now again she lay down.
   Soon now it is dawn;
   Now Grizzly Woman fell asleep,
        Water Bug arose;
   Now she cast t'áLmu t'áLmu on her,   (she numbed her)
        She slept.

IX. [Grizzly Woman escaped]
A   She told them,
      "Quickly! Get up!"
   They got up,
      they hurried;
   They went down to their canoes,
      they got on them.
B   She ran,
      she fetched their paddles,
         she put *all* of them in—
            her older sister's paddles had holes—
            now they went.
C   They are going,
      they turned to look,
         now she is pursuing them there.
   She curses Water Bug:
      "So that is why you came!
   You tell the people lies."
   She gets close to them,
      she took her snot,
         she threw it at them:
            their paddles broke.
D   She pursued them;
      she will get close to them;
         she will blow her nose,
            she will throw her snot at them;
               their paddles will break;
                  all the paddles they brought,
                  all became broken.
E   Now they have gotten close (to their village);
      now she took out her (older sister's) paddles;
         in vain she threw her snot at them;
            there it will go right through them;
               they go.
X.   [Grizzly Woman destroyed]
A   The people said,
      "Something (is wrong).
   A canoe is coming,
      hurrying this way."
   They went out,
      they said,
         "Seems like our chief's wife pursues them."

They got their bows, their arrows.
They arrived,
    Water Bug ran,
        she told their older brother (the chief):
            "She consumes people.
            She has taken along a certain number,
            She kills them all.
            She pursues us."
Now they waited for her.

B   Soon,
        she came ashore,
            now they shot at her.
    She would tell them,
        "Goodness! Why does Water Bug just lie and lie to you?"
    She is *going*,
        they shoot at her.

C   Her husband sat on top of the house,
        he shot at her;
    She is close to him there,
        now he has only one arrow.
    He thought,
        "Never mind!"
    He threw it at her (shot it despairingly),
        he wounded her little finger,
            it split,
                there she fell,
                    he had killed her.
    In truth there she put her heart,
        in her little finger.

D   Now they burned her;
        he got all of her,
            they ground up her bones;
                they blew them (ashes) away.

E   Now they went,
        they went to gather up the corpses,
            they arrived.
    There they went ashore,
        they took Water Bug along,
            she showed them the whole place there;
        they arrived,
            where the first ones (were),
                now black,
                    rotting;
        they took them *all* to the canoes.

Now they were taken to their graveyard,
they buried them *all*,
they ceased
All done.

Story story.

The Grizzly Woman is named with *a-* for the first time in the midst of the third of the five times that she persuades women of a village to go to gather camas roots with her.

An overview of the naming of Grizzly Woman in this text seems to show two culminating arcs. One ends in the naming of her with *a-* in the third trip, the other in the interaction with Water Bug in the fifth, where she is named seven times, one of them again with *a-*.

The first series has to do with her deception and killing of her women victims. When she comes to the village headman to be his wife at the outset of the story, she is not named. Neither is she named in the course of the first trip, when she lures women away from the village in hopes of camas, then kills them. She is named for the first time, and twice, in the course of the second trip. After all have arrived, she tells the second group that their predecessors must have gone to a place where there is even more camas. She advises them to stay where they are for the night. Having gone off as if to visit the first group of women (actually slain), Grizzly Woman (p. 157, 1. 18) is named for the first time in the story when she returns to say that the others have lots of camas, and had said they would eat it where they were. After the second group eat and finish their meal, she is named again (p. 158, 1. 1): "Grizzly Woman is not there." Then they hear singing, and soon she returns, saying, "Why are you silent? They are singing yonder." The women reply that they had heard, and begin to sing too.

In the course of the third trip, Grizzly Woman is named a third time at the same point of deception. She comes to the women and says, "Why are you silent?" (p. 159, 1. 2). Then, she is named twice more, once when she lies down to sleep with the others, and once when she arises to kill them.

There is something grimly grotesque in finding Grizzly Woman in the role of community organizer and sing-along leader, as it were. To go gathering roots, or berries, was one of the most enjoyable activities of women, a social occasion as well as a practical necessity. In pursuit of her deception, the one who is using an activity of group enjoyment as a cover for mass murder exerts herself to maintain the appearances of group enjoyment.

Through the sequence of trips there emerges a current of increasing suspicion and uneasiness, calling for greater exertion on Grizzly Woman's part, both as mistress of ceremonies and as user of spirit power. From the first to third trips there is a development, both in the steps she takes to deceive the women before nightfall, and in the expression of her exertion of the special spirit-power by which she makes them sleep, dead to the world, so that she can kill them all without detection during the night.

On the first trip, the text is terse. There is no need to deceive the first group about predecessors, and the use of spirit-power is not named, but expressed through a sentence fragment and a causative suffix (II A–C; p. 157, ll. 1–9).

After Grizzly Woman is named in regard to her reporting on the preceding group, and with regard to going off to deceive the new group by pretending to be the first group singing, the account of the second trip introduces the word for her special spirit-power for inducing sleep (III D; p. 158, ll. 7–10). The line translated "she numbed them (with her spirit-power)" contains the verb phrase *t'áLmu* past (*ga-*) she (*g-*) them (*L*) do (*-u-x*), she did *t'áLmu* to them.

On the third trip, after Grizzly Woman has falsely reported about predecessors, the women stop digging and think, "It's not as it should be. Something somehow (is wrong)." (IV ii A; p. 158, l. 20, through p. 159, l. 1). Shortly Grizzly (named) gets there (p. 159, l. 2) and asks, as with the second group, "Why are you so silent?" She adds that the women yonder (actually slain) are singing, giggling, laughing, and have baked their camas where they are. The women say they are just beginning to feel queer. Grizzly replies, "Oh dear, why? Soon they will be dancing again. Suppose I go see them again." Soon they hear singing, and when she returns, she tells them to sing too. They agree, and attempt to sing, but no, they quit (as shown in the presentation of this passage earlier).

It is in this third trip that it is mentioned for the first time that Grizzly Woman lies down to sleep with the others. She may have lain down in the first two trips as well; mention now has to do, not with description, but dramatic tension. She has deceived the second and third groups by false report and singing, but in the face of the first explicit uneasiness, and the failure of the attempt to sing, must add a third explicit step. She lies down to sleep as $\emptyset$-, and gets up as *a-kitsimani* (in IV iii–iv; p. 159, ll. 10–14).

The contrast between the passive state, lying down to sleep, and the active state, arising to kill them all, is parallel to the contrast found with the alternation of *wa-* and *a-*. The parallel suggests that in a text in which the terms of alternation are *a-* : $\emptyset$-, the overt element *a-* stands in the same relation to $\emptyset$-, as does *wa-* to *a-*. In summary form, there appears to be a proportion:

wa- :*a-* :: *a-* :$\emptyset$-.

It is natural to Chinookan rhetoric to have a culmination in a third scene of a series, and that is what seems to be the case here. Along with the introduction of *a-* in the contrast between Grizzly Woman as deceptive partner in sleep, and as user of sleep to kill, there is a doubling of the word for the power she uses. In the Clackamas the eighth line in the passage just quoted is *"t'áLmu t'áLmu gagELuX."*

The fourth trip seems in tone both a development and a preparation. It continues the growth of suspicion and uneasiness. As soon as the fourth group of women arrive, one begins crying. Asked why she is making a bad omen for herself, she replies, "No, something is wrong, something happened to our people at the place you see." Others dismiss her fear; but when she tries to dig, she cries again. In the evening the women say they will not build a fire (because of their worry). It is then that Grizzly Woman comes, presumably from having pretended to visit the groups that had come already. This is the one point in the scene in which she is named ($\emptyset$- in V ii B; p. 160, l. 7). She asks what is the matter, is told that one is ill, and says she will soon stop being sick.

Surprised that the women are already lying down for sleep, Grizzly Woman is told that they will dig the next day, and says she will go to tell the others (actually already slain). The women do not attend, but soon hear singing. One says, "Do you suppose it is really so?" There is no mention of an attempt on their own part to sing. Returning, Grizzly Woman says the supposedly still alive others had been going to come, but she had told them the fourth group was already lying down to sleep. Extending the mention of her lying down herself in the third trip, she says,

"Now I will lie down too," and, the text continues, now she lay down.

At this point the wording is almost the same as in the third trip (V iv; p. 160, l. 19, through p. 161, line 1). There is a diminution in the expressive weight of the passage in that Grizzly Woman is not named at all, whereas she had been named twice in the corresponding passage of the third trip; and that she killed them all is left unstated. The impact of naming Grizzly Woman is shown in the use of the device in the second and third trips with regard to deception of the women about their predecessors. Naming her in the context of the deception and death of sleep is reserved for the intermediate climax, the third trip, and the major climax and reversal of the whole story on the fifth.

(Enter Water Bug.) The growing uneasiness was collective in the third trip, and individuated as well, and anonymously, in the fourth. It is crystallized in a decisive heroine in the fifth trip, which becomes the whole of a second part. (Such extraposition of a culminating fifth step of a series is a major feature of Louis Simpson's "Deserted Boy" as well,[4] and may have been a general device of Chinookan narrative art.) When the others at the village say they will go with Grizzly Woman in the morning, a young girl, Water Bug, insists on going along. Grizzly Bear does not want her to. In point of fact, "When a little girl was especially intelligent and perceptive, older people might refer to her, during the years when she was still very small, as *amaLk'wilkwiq*. This is the name of a flat water bug which although very quiet sometimes bites" (p. 284, n. 168). Grizzly Woman was presumably aware of this potentiality, and there is a sustained spoken exchange over the issue between her, Water Bug, and Water Bug's older sister. In the next scene, Grizzly Woman is named, once with ∅ (in VI A) and once with *a-* (in VI B); the full passage is in VI A–B; p. 161, ll. 12–16.

The significance of the second naming of Grizzly Woman, the naming with *a-*, is its connection with the turning point of the action. Heretofore Grizzly Woman has been successful in the pretense that everything is all right, that the women who had preceded (after the first) are farther away, rolling in camas, as it were, and singing before they sleep. After causing them magically to sleep, and killing them, she has hidden their bodies and their paddles, all in the same place. The hiding of the paddles has followed the killing. In this fifth and culminating trip, she has intended to take the paddles in advance, apparently to preclude escape and flight by canoe. Which is just what will happen. Not only are paddles necessary to the canoes, *all* the paddles are necessary, for in the event, Grizzly Woman in pursuit succeeds in breaking all but the last paddles by hurling her nasal mucous at them. Close to home, Water Bug takes out her older sister's paddles, the only ones remaining; and they reach home because these paddles have holes, and the nasal mucous goes right through.

That Grizzly Woman forgets Water Bug and forgets the paddles, then, is the turning point that leads to her downfall. The Clackamas verb, translated here "forget," has the same stem as in the word for the fact that Water Bug pays no attention a little earlier, but in a different construction. The verbal contrast highlights, perhaps humorously, the contrast between little girl and murderous ogress.

The naming of Grizzly Woman at the turning point that leads to the success of her antagonist is analogous to the naming of her at the turning point in another story, the adventure of Old Watcheeno's father (text 134). In both stories the explicit naming seems to underscore the identity of the ogress and to heighten the ensuing success of escape. In both stories, indeed, the title identifies the Grizzly Ogress with *wa-*, but *wa-* does not occur in the text. In "Grizzly Woman Pursued Him," the creature is referred to only by a pronominal prefix until the proper name is introduced with *a-* at the turning point. In this story of "Grizzly Woman Killed People," she is named a number of times, but only with the zero noun prefix, except for the description of the central action in the third trip (discussed above), and here at the turning point in the fifth.

These parallels between the two texts seem striking to me. The parallelism is reinforced by attention to the location of the explicit naming of Grizzly Women. Although the sums are disproportionate (thirteen namings in this text, one in that of Old Watcheeno's father), the locations are not. Of the thirteen namings in "Grizzly Woman Began to Kill People," seven are in the account of the fifth and last trip, and five of the seven are in the crucial scene involving sleep. It is the counterpart of the scene involving sleep from the third trip presented above but with the opposite outcome. Water Bug has discovered the corpses of the women

Grizzly Woman had killed, and shared the knowledge, first with her older sister, then with the other women. Each time those who are told weep and then wash their faces to avoid suspicion. Grizzly Woman does accuse Water Bug of lying to the people about something, while proceeding herself to say that the other women (now known to be dead) are drying their cooked camas. When she leaves them, Water Bug instructs the people, again, to watch carefully, that she (Water Bug) is the one Grizzly Woman intends to kill first, that they will leave her when she has fallen asleep. She then gets shells from the river (presumably to protect her eyes against Grizzly Woman's magic). The story proceeds in an act in which namings of Grizzly Woman are concentrated and concluded (VIII).

The concentration of the namings of Grizzly Woman in this passage is hardly accidental, nor, I think, is the fact that the sum of namings is the pattern number, five. This scene is the great reversal scene. As we have seen on the first trip, it is briefly, if effectively, presented that the women are caused to sleep. On the second, the spirit-power, *t'aɬmu,* is named once, and in the third, reduplicated. It is reduplicated in the fourth trip as well. In the fifth trip it is reduplicated twice, once when used (to no avail) and heard by Water Bug, a second time when used by Water Bug herself! The sequence of the five namings of Grizzly Woman tell the story in themselves:

> Grizzly Woman said, "Now I too now I lie down in bed."
> Grizzly Woman arose slowly, silently.
> Now again Grizzly Woman got up.
> Now Grizzly Woman became sleepy.
> Now Grizzly Woman fell asleep.

It may be significant that Grizzly Woman is not named again beyond this point.

A consideration of the reversal in this scene goes together with consideration of the other concentration of namings that it shows, the namings of young Water Bug. She is named sixteen times in this last part of the myth, eleven times in the section just discussed. (The remaining five occur in the successful flight back to the village and the killing of Grizzly Woman by her headman-husband, Water Bug's older brother.) The concentration in itself shows the emergence into the text of a new motivation, focused

on the young girl. Four of the sixteen namings are with *wa-*,
rather than *a-*, and these are revealing as well.

The first naming of Water Bug is in the scene which we have
seen to be the beginning of the end for Grizzly Woman, when she
forgets Water Bug and forgets the paddles. Water Bug is named
when she comes on stage, as it were, with *a-* (VI A; p. 161, l. 12),
but is named with *wa-* when she takes the paddles (VI B; p. 161,
l. 17). It is at that same point that Grizzly Woman is named for
the second time in the long story with *a-*. This conjunction of the
two stronger prefixes for the two actors at the peripety of the
story seems no accident.

The other three times at which Water Bug is named with *wa-*
each involves her as the crucial opponent of Grizzly Woman.
When she speaks to the people as to what to do, after she has
disclosed the murder of their companions, she is named with *a-*.
When Grizzly Woman then comes and asks, "What are you being
quiet about? You have lied to the people about something or
other, Water Bug!" she names her with *wa-*. This naming introduces a recurrent theme, for Grizzly Woman will several times try
to convince others that the trouble is all lies spread by Water Bug,
even when she addresses her headman-husband in the village,
having pursued the escaping women there. The next naming of
Water Bug with *wa-* is in the night. When the fire has gone down a
little, and Grizzly Woman arises stealthily, she goes first to Water
Bug and her sister, and looks at Water Bug (*wa-*) (p. 163, l. 10).
Finally, Water Bug is named with *wa-* when the women escape and
Grizzly Woman begins to follow them. The text states: "She was
pursuing Water Bug. So that is why you came! You lied to the
people" (p. 164, l. 15).

Each of the four namings of Water Bug with *wa-* introduces
and expresses a crucial element in the struggle between them:
(1) the hiding of the paddles, forgotten by Grizzly Woman, which
will later permit escape; (2) the telling of the people the truth
about the deaths of their companions, which Grizzly Woman
senses and tries to stamp as lies; (3) invulnerability to Grizzly
Woman's power of causing sleep; (4) escape afterward back to
their own village. The demise of Grizzly Woman is accomplished,
no doubt appropriately in Chinookan terms, by a man, Water
Bug's closest older male relative. That any women are saved at
all, and that Grizzly Woman can be killed, is the culmination

of Water Bug's overcoming of her in each of the four respects just listed.

This connection between naming with *wa-* and confrontation reinforces the interpretation of the point of naming Grizzly Woman in "Grizzly Woman Pursued Him" (text 134), and of the concentration of Grizzly Bear naming in this same, fifth section of the present myth.

Naming and Prefix-Alternation as Foregrounding

The stories involving Grizzly Woman suggest a hierarchy of expressive alternatives. It is possible to relate a story in Chinookan without naming an actor at all. If the identity can be taken for granted, the person-marking prefixes of the verb will suffice for the roles of the actor in narrative action. Should an actor be named, it is theoretically possible to have the stem without a prefix; to have one of the common third-person singular prefixes; or to have a prefix preceded by *w-*.

The order in which the alternatives have been listed would seem to be the order of increasing characterization and dramatization. That *w-* is at the top of the hierarchy seems indicated by its exclusive use when Grizzly Woman is named in titles, and by the role it has been seen to play, both with Grizzly Woman and with Water Bug. A full study of Clackamas usage for all myth actors is needed, but I think these conclusions from the study of Grizzly Woman texts will be borne out by the rest of what we have of Clackamas from Mrs. Howard. The weighting and dramatic point of the narratives will be found to involve the stylistic choice of whether and where to name, and if to name, and then how. Concentration of naming and choice of prefix provide foregrounding in the text and express underlying conceptions of identity as well.

An attentive reader may ask: If these relations of alternation *within* the texts are correct, what about the alternation *among* texts? What about the alternation between kinds of alternation? Why *wa-* : *a-* in some stories, and *a-* : *∅-* in others?

The use of a zero prefix in the myth that ends with Grizzly Woman's encounter with Water Bug might seem to fit the fact that she attempts to deceive others throughout the myth. Perhaps zero prefix goes with concealment of identity. But there is no disguise of identity in the other myth with the zero prefix for her. Furthermore, when Grizzly Woman attempts to disguise herself drastically in another identity, even donning another woman's skin in the myth of Gitskux and his older brother, she is never named with a zero prefix.

Eating versus Only Killing

There is an explanation of the occurrence of the zero prefix in the corpus we have if a statement of Mrs. Howard's grandmother can be taken as metaphorical, rather than literal. In the course of the story of Gitskux, it may be recalled, Mrs. Howard reported that her grandmother would intervene to say that the Grizzly Woman in question was the only one who eats people (p. 320, l. 14). That seemed a reason for connecting her particularly with the girl who becomes a Grizzly Woman in another story told by the grandmother, "Grizzly Bear and Black Bear Ran Away with the Two Girls." The connection indeed seems valid because of the many similarities, including the eating of people. But careful attention to other stories shows the Grizzly Woman actors to be associated with humans as food in almost every one!

There is no such association in "Coon and Coyote Went and Stole" (text 3), which, as has been said, is a recent extension of the Grizzly Woman identity to the two sisters who hoard fish. And they are never individually identified, but always treated as dual (is-). In "Coyote Went around the Land" (text 9), Coyote saves women from becoming the food prepared by Grizzly Woman for her husband. "Grizzly Bear and Black Bear Ran Away with the Two Girls" (text 14) has just been mentioned. In "Thunder and His Mother" (text 30), the Grizzly Women encountered prepare "earth stew" containing human bones. "Gitskux and His Older Brother" (text 34) has just been mentioned. In "Kusaydi and His Older Brother" (text 40), the Grizzly Women again prepare "earth stew."

Besides the two short explanatory texts (texts 143, 144), there remain just three. In none of these does a Grizzly Woman eat humans or her own kind, and in none of these texts is she named with the prefix wa-.

In "Grizzly Woman Began to Kill People" (text 17), she is said only to kill the successive groups of women. In "Cock Robin . . ." (text 31), the danger is only said to be that she will kill the two brothers. In "Grizzly Woman Pursued Him" (text 134), the indicated danger is presumably death.

This correlation suggests that the full Grizzly Woman character did include the eating of humans or her own kin; that *wa-* is associated with the full character of Grizzly Woman; and that the absence of *wa-* in texts in which the eating of humans or kin is not in question is not accident, but appropriateness.

The statement by Mrs. Howard's grandmother makes still a certain sense. Only in the myth in which she makes the statement ("Gitskux" [text 34]), and the myth with which we have connected it (text 14), does a Grizzly Woman enter into a kinship, indeed a nuclear-family relationship with human beings, only to eat them later.[5] The other stories have the obtaining of human food anonymously or offstage.

Frequency of Alternation and Personal Concern

The dramatistic rightness of the grandmother's statement goes together with an interesting statistic. Prefix alternation is not all that common in the texts in which it occurs. If the five texts are tallied, excluding titles, the result is as follows:

Text	*wa-*	*a-*	$\emptyset$-
(9)	1	1	
(16)	9	1	
(34)	9	5	
(17)		2	11
(31)		1	1

We should note in passing that the tally shows *a-* to be always the marked case. In text 9 there is a simple before-and-after difference in the state of Grizzly Woman, danger : no danger, to which perhaps (31) can be seen as analogous. In text 16, *a-* is used at the one point at which Grizzly Woman has become inactive. Conversely, in keeping with the scale suggested earlier, *a-* is used in text 17 at two culminating points of her identity, as against the common use of $\emptyset$-.

The story of Gitskux (text 34) fits the semantic pattern established for *wa-* : *a-*, but it stands out as the only story in which alternation is at all common. As the tally shows, only one other story has as many as two uses of the marked alternative, and the concluding encounter with Water Bug becomes a full narrative in itself there.

The appropriateness of alternation in the story of Gitskux is understandable in comparison with the two other stories in which *wa-*, expressing the full characterization of Grizzly Woman, alternates with *a-*. The story involving Coyote (text 9) has Coyote come, Lone Ranger like, to the rescue of a group of women. The Grizzly Ogress is hardly on stage, and not named when she is. The story of "Black Bear and Grizzly Bear" (text 16) is a gripping drama, sister killing sister, and cousins killing cousins in revenge; but it is set among bears, and much of the attention is focused on the successful escape of Black Bear's children. Once the action is set in motion, the mother anticipating her death and advising the sons, the success of the sons under the leadership of Wasguk-mayli can be anticipated.

The story of "Gitskux and His Older Brother" is the one story of the three that has a periodic character. The plot is extended, not by escape and journey, but by the repeated return of the Ogress thought safely dead. The drama, perhaps nightmare, of the monstrous figure who comes uninvited, kills the proper wife and dons her skin, comes back and comes back. And where the children of Black Bear conduct a heroic and humorous escape, the children of Gitskux's older brother are shushed, stay away from their father in fright, have their pet taken, have a pet killed, see their mother killed in fighting begun for their sake, and finally are killed and eaten with the rest of their village. To be sure, the corresponding pair of nephews in the later marriage of the elder brother survive; but the children of the first marriage are a continuing witness, and eventual casualty, of the first two comings of Wakitsimani.

The unique frequency of alternation between active and passive prefixes for the Grizzly Ogress in this story reinforces the inference that the Ogress was of special concern to Mrs. Howard's grandmother. It is as if sensitivity to the expressive possibility of the alternation reflected a sensitivity to the instability latent within personality within the home. The story is in effect a dramatization of the difference between a would-be wife (Grizzly Woman) and true wives, the first and second wives of Gitskux. More than that, it is a dramatization of the contrast between failure and success in integrating the "masculine" components (aggression, strength) and the "feminine" components of personality. The first wife is strong, bringing in deer that her husband kills with one hand; the second wife is a paragon of both strength and spiritual power. Grizzly Woman tries to emulate each and fails each time.

The other story with more than one alternation is that of "Grizzly Woman Began to Kill People"; and if we extend our consideration to the use of naming itself, together with prefix alternation, it is rich too, as we have seen. Moreover, it also suggests concern with the integration of "masculine" and "feminine" components of personality. It does so especially in imagery.

In the story of Seal,[6] the daughter emerges from the darkness of the scenes to light, herself building the fire and raising the torch that discovers her uncle's murder. (Whereas Water Bug is able to build a fire in advance to prevent murder—and arises and builds it in the same words as Seal's daughter.) Seal's daughter is associated with symbolic wetness: she first hears that the uncle's wife must be a disguised man because of the sound made when all go outside at night to urinate. She then feels something wet dropping at night onto her underneath the bed of her uncle and his "wife." Her mother sets it aside as the result of intercourse; it turns out to be her uncle's blood. At the end she weeps three times, framing her remonstrance to her mother and her lament for her uncle. This imagery seems to me to express her emergence into sexual awareness and maturity as an individual: from darkness to light; from hearing one product of a phallus at a distance, to feeling what is taken to be another such product in bed (but it is blood); to herself producing tears, while assuming the right to remonstrate.

The imagery associated with Grizzly Woman and Water Bug is of quite a different kind. Grizzly Woman inveigles the women into going off to use their digging sticks to get camas bulbs. While they are away from the village, she kills them at night with an arrow-spear. When Water Bug does not sleep, she accuses her of being concerned about young men who might come to her older sister. Water Bug herself says that she has dreamed of a bloody arrow-spear. Grizzly Woman is killed by the last arrow of Water Bug's older brother. Danger and death are rather closely associated with long pointed things. Safety, on the other hand, is mediated by things that are long but not so pointed: paddles. The safest paddles of all are those that are not intact, but have holes (presumably from use), those of an elder sister. All this strongly suggests an opposition in terms of phallic symbolism. The opposition seems to express a contrast between the danger of sex outside, away, as against the safety of sex that is more domestic, more muted. Arrow-spears versus paddles, as it were.

Let us look more closely at the scene of flight and escape. The nasal mucous that Grizzly Woman casts can perhaps be associated with the body's other secretion from a longitudinal part with an opening, semen. That fits the consistent character of the other images associated with Grizzly Woman, just noted. The elder sister's paddles seem a dual image. The fact that they have holes might imply an association with the female organ. Grizzly Woman casts an obnoxious surrogate of semen; but the escaping women, having implements that contain a surrogate of the female organ, are invulnerable. The unity, or integration, of attributes of the two genders is the means of safety. The presence of the holes does not seem to exclude the phallic symbolism. Not only are the paddles long, but the women insert them as steadily and rapidly as they can into the water. It may be the unity, or integration, of attributes of the two genders that expresses the means of safety.

The third story in which naming is frequent, that of Black Bear and Grizzly Woman and their children, is a direct confrontation between Grizzly Woman and a mother with her children, which fits with the fact that it is a child, a young girl, Water Bug, who overcomes Grizzly Woman in the story discussed here, and fits also with the significant witnessing by children in the story of Gitskux.

It is particularly in myths from Mrs. Howard's grandmother that there is a focus on the Grizzly Woman figure as more than a well-known ogress and danger; a use of naming, prefix alternation, and imagery to express a failure of the integration of "masculine" and "feminine" qualities in a woman, and a delineation of the effect on girls of the situations that result. Concentration of naming and choice of prefix do indeed provide foregrounding in texts and do express underlying conceptions of identity. The use of an alternation almost unnoticeable, and easy enough to dismiss, is thus found to say something of fundamental concern about women, and about girls growing up to be women, in both traditional and acculturationally shattered society.

Notes

1. This paper stems from a study of all the Clackamas Chinook narratives having to do with the Grizzly Ogress. That study is in turn part of a book-length manuscript, "Bears That Save and Destroy." Portions of the manuscript are adapted for the present paper; the analysis into verse of the entire story of "Grizzly Woman Began to Kill People" has been done especially for this paper. Only the English text, revised from the translation first published by Jacobs (*Clackamas Chinook Texts, Part 1*), is given here, for reasons of economy of space and typography. Charles Bigelow and I have in preparation a book that is to present a series of Chinookan texts in the original languages, according to the kind of verse analysis shown here, and employing a typography devised by Bigelow.

The method of verse analysis has been first presented in two papers (Dell Hymes, "Louis Simpson's 'The Deserted Boy,'" *Poetics* 5, no. 2 [1976]: 119-55; and idem, "Discovering Oral Performance and Measured Verse in American Indian Narrative," *New Literary History* 8, no. 3 [1977]: 431-57), elaborated in another (idem, "Verse Analysis of a Wasco Text," to appear in *International Journal of American Linguistics*, 1980), and exemplified in another paper and book-length manuscript (idem, "Myth as Verse," manuscript; and idem, "Victoria Howard's Gitskux and His Older Brother," to appear in a volume edited by Brian Swann, in press).

The four basic works by Jacobs on Clackamas Chinook are as follows: Melville Jacobs, *Clackamas Chinook Texts, Part 1*, Indiana University Research Center in Anthropology, Folklore, and Linguistics, Publication 8 (Bloomington, 1958); idem, *Content and Style of an Oral Literature* (Chicago: University of Chicago Press, 1958); idem, *Clackamas Chinook Texts, Part 2*, Indiana University Publications in Anthropology, Folklore, and Linguistics, Publication 8 (Bloomington, 1959); and idem, *The People Are Coming Soon: Analyses of Clackamas Chinook Myths and Tales* (Seattle: University of Washington Press, 1960).

Text and page and line numbers in the following discussion refer to *Clackamas Chinook Texts*, parts 1 and 2. Text and page numbering is consecutive throughout the two volumes.

2. A word on the verbs in the original of this passage for those who wish to pursue issues raised here: *ga-L-u-ya* and *ga-L-a-sk-u-pq* both begin with the remote past *ga-* that is common in myths; *L-* identifies Gitskux, his brother, and his two nephews (in such cases, the indefiniteness of *L-* can convey informality, a lack of social distance); *-a-Sk-* in the second verb is an old indirect object construction with postposition for entering a house; *-u-* is the unmarked directional element "from here to there" before the stem; *-ya* is "to go, come," and *-pq* is "to enter." The third verb, that with Akicimani, has the zero tense prefix and a stative suffix, *-t*. The third person feminine prefix for an intransitive subject, *s-*, drops regularly before /u/; the *u-* is again the unmarked directional; *-X* is the factotum verb stem of all work. The third verb quite literally designates Akicimani as in a state of being (there).

When Chinookan words are cited, I have followed certain conventions in order to avoid special type. All involve substituting capital letters for diacritics or symbols not conventional in English spelling.

C = usual c with superposed wedge (like "ch" in English *hatch*)
E = usual upside down minuscule e (Hebrew *schwa*, with range of vowel in English *just*)
G = usual g with subposed dot (a velar voiced stop)
L = usual l with line through it ("voiceless l," like "ll" in Welsh *Lloyd*)
S = usual s with superposed wedge (like "sh" in English *hash*)
X = usual x with subposed dot (a velar voiceless fricative, as in German *ach*)

3. The format and basis of this translation are discussed in detail in Hymes, "Louis Simpson's 'The Deserted Boy'"; and idem, "Discovering Oral Performance and Measured Verse in American Indian Narrative."

4. See my discussion in "Louis Simpson's 'The Deserted Boy.'"

5. And in text 14, the figure is not explicitly named as *kitsimani*, but only referred to, first by her own name, and then as having become a "dangerous being," *a-qSXiLau.*

6. See my essay "Discovering Oral Performance."

Index

For the benefit of readers unfamiliar with the materials of American Indian literatures, this selective index focuses primarily on essays and books most germane to texts and critical commentaries.